Gardeners' World Vegetable Book

Geoff Hamilton

D1324189

BRITISH BROADCASTING CORPORATION

Contents

Published by the
British Broadcasting Corporation
35 Marylebone High Street
London W1M 4AA

ISBN 0 563 17962 7
First published 1981
© Geoff Hamilton 1981
Drawings by Lorna Turpin

Printed in Great Britain by
Thomson Litho Ltd, East Kilbride, Scotland

Author's Introduction

Gardening has never been an exact science. Ask ten good gardeners how they achieve their results, and you will almost certainly get ten different answers. And they will all be right! There's no doubt about it, we all have our own pet methods and if they work for us we are unlikely to change them in a hurry. Controversy always rages and that's one of the factors that makes gardening such a fascinating and absorbing hobby.

But, when it falls to your lot to advise others seriously, you must at least be as exact as possible. And that is one of the primary functions of the *Gardeners' World* trials ground at Barnsdale. On those two acres we endeavour to test pet theories, to try out new products and methods, to evaluate the results of the plant breeders' art, and to adapt modern, scientific methods to suit the home gardener.

This book is intended to set out the results of the experiments we have conducted for *Gardeners' World* in rather more detail than is possible on the programme.

With a few notable exceptions, gardening techniques have changed little since Victorian times. Pick up almost any gardening book, and you will find references to 'the herbaceous border', 'the rock garden', and 'the shrub border'. The illustrations consist of massive vistas of plants at Blenheim Palace, Chatsworth or Kew.

Well, gardening may not have changed, but gardens certainly have. Over the years, with houses being built closer and closer together, gardens have shrunk to a fraction of their previous size. There simply isn't space any more for gardening on a grandiose scale. With less space and time at their disposal gardeners must look for ways of increasing their productivity. Every spare inch of land must be used to its fullest advantage. And nowhere is this more important than in the vegetable garden.

With this in mind, perhaps the top priority on the vegetable trials at Barnsdale is to find methods of increasing yields per unit area of land.

There are four ways we can do this, and we have been trying to expand our knowledge of them all. First of all, we have looked at new cultivation techniques designed to increase yields without putting up costs. Then we have tried simply to cram more crops into a given space, mainly by the new 'Deep-bed' method described in the first chapter. We also grow as many new varieties as we can; plant breeding has taken tremendous strides forward in the last ten years and there are now varieties available to the amateur gardener which will out-crop anything we have seen before. Finally, we have tried various methods of extending the season at both ends in an effort to reduce to a minimum the amount of time the land is vacant.

Of course, not all our experiments are successful. We have had a few notable failures, but we can glean valuable information from these too.

Of course, we do not claim that our experiments at Barnsdale are in any way scientific. We have neither the facilities nor the expertise for that. I like to look upon them as 'gardeners' trials'. But we do get a great deal of valuable help and information from the government research stations throughout the country. Notable amongst these is the National Vegetable Research Station with whom we have a close liaison. Their work is, of course, mainly for the commercial grower, but it is often possible to adapt commercial techniques to the smaller scale of the back-yard garden. There are many such examples within this book.

While I feel strongly that hobby gardening should retain much of the traditional methods that make it so enjoyable, there is a lot to be gained from modern technology. And there is no happier gardener than a successful one.

Geoff Hamilton
Barnsdale, 1981

The Deep-Bed Method

There can be no doubt that the biggest limitation for today's gardener is space. Even with acres of land, the keen gardener never seems to have enough room for everything he wants to do. With gardens getting smaller and smaller it's even more difficult to know where to cram everything in.

The problem is even more acute for the vegetable grower. Few gardeners wish to turn their whole plot over to vegetables, but if we are to provide the family with fresh produce all the year round, there seems little alternative.

With this in mind, we have turned over part of our trials ground at Barnsdale to investigate a revolutionary new method of growing vegetables that has enabled us to increase dramatically our yields per square yard.

1. *Measuring with two garden lines*

Known as the 'Deep-Bed Method', the system saves space, time and effort and certainly costs no more than conventional methods. On a very much larger scale, agricultural scientists at Luddington Research Station have been experimenting on similar lines.

They too, have evidence of greatly increased yields following deep cultivation. A certain amount of work has also been done in the United States, though I remain a little sceptical of their claims which suggest that the system will increase crops by up to four times. We are a little more modest, claiming only to double the yields per square yard when compared with conventional methods.

I have to admit that there is one major disadvantage. The construction of a deep-bed does involve double-digging, and that is hard work at the best of times. But once that job is done it should not have to be repeated more than once every three to five years, depending on your soil. And the rest of the normal vegetable garden chores will be greatly reduced.

2. *Marking out the first trench with a 2ft cane*

Because plants are grown closer together, they soon cover the soil depriving weeds of space and light, so that the normal incessant task of hoeing or hand pulling weeds is cut to a minimum.

Because the beds are never walked upon after digging, the soil remains loose and uncompacted. This means that once a crop has been harvested all that is necessary before sowing or planting the next, is to rake over the top couple of inches. There will be no need to dig for the rest of the season.

One unexpected bonus I found was that the beds seem to be much easier to control. Perhaps because the rows are short, and the less interesting work is cut to a minimum, *the work gets done*. And at the right time, too. But undoubtedly the greatest advantage is the bumper harvest these beds produce. They will certainly double production yard for yard, and in some cases we tripled our harvests quite easily.

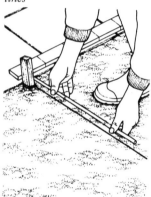

3. *Digging out the soil from the first spade's depth*

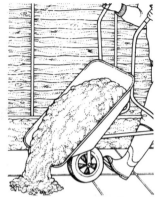

4. *Taking away the soil*

5. *A clean spade makes for easier work*

6. *Clean loose soil from the bottom of the trench*

Most vegetables seem to thrive under deep-bed conditions, though I found little advantage in growing such things as runner or climbing french beans this way. The good gardener would prepare for these crops in much the same way anyhow.

The soil at Barnsdale is light and sandy and in the first season I found some problems with the increased drainage. In dry weather, I had to water practically every day. I have solved this one now by working a little manure into the top few inches of the bed to help retain moisture. But on heavy land, the increased drainage could be a real boon. In countries with very high levels of rainfall, nearly all vegetable crops are grown on raised beds for this very reason. So, if your soil is a heavy clay, deep-bed growing will go a long way towards solving your problems.

Making a deep-bed
The golden rule of deep-bed growing is never to tread on the soil after the initial digging. All the work is done from the paths either side. So, the width of the bed will depend upon how far you can reach. In our first year, I made the beds 5 ft (1.5 m.) wide. That was a mistake. I found it quite uncomfortable to reach to the middle and was continually tempted to ease my aching back by putting a foot in the middle of the bed. The alternative would have been to employ a gorilla!

The second season, the beds were cut down to 4 ft (1.2 m.) wide and this was ideal. There is no reason at all why they should not be even narrower, so before you start work see how far you can reach comfortably, and make the beds twice this width.

Another point to bear in mind is the length of the bed. Working from the side paths means that you will be continually walking round the bed. So, unless you really enjoy an afternoon's 'constitutional', don't make the beds too long. If, for some reason, the shape or size of your vegetable plot makes a long bed desirable, make provision for a cross path in the middle. It will save quite a lot of time.

Mark out the bed accurately before you start digging, with two tight garden lines (1).

Double-digging a deep-bed is no different from conventional double-digging, except that the rows will only be as long as the width of the bed.

Start by cutting a cane 2 ft (60 cm.) long. This will be used to mark the width of each trench. It is important to do this, since it will help you dig the bed level throughout.

Measure out the first trench with the cane (2), and stick it in one corner as a marker. Then dig out the soil from the top spit (spade's depth) (3). This should be put into a wheelbarrow and carted to the other end of the bed, preferably piling it on the path (4). This soil will be used to fill the last trench when you finally reach it.

The bottom of the trench is now broken up to the full depth of the fork (7). When you do this avoid bringing up the subsoil. There is no need to turn the soil over, or even to lift it out. Simply push the fork in, pull the shaft back towards you and work it around a bit to ensure that any hard 'pan' is thoroughly broken.

On top of this, put in a good layer of well-rotted manure (8). In a trench 4 ft × 2 ft (1.2 m. × 60 cm.), you'll need something like a quarter of a barrow full. If you can't get hold of farmyard manure, there are several alternatives that are perhaps more readily available in your area. Spent mushroom manure is ideal. This can often be obtained quite cheaply from the local mushroom farm, especially if you are prepared to go and collect it in bags. Alternatively, use spent hop manure, wool shoddy or, as a last resort because it's expensive, coarse moss peat.

7. *Break up the soil a full fork's depth*

Well-rotted garden compost is also excellent, but you'll need quite a lot of it and most gardeners with a small patch find it difficult to produce enough.

The next 2 ft (60 cm.) trench can now be marked out and dug in just the same way. This time though, the soil is thrown forward to fill the first trench (9). You'll find that the broken-down soil will fill more of a space than when compacted, so the dug part will be several inches higher than the rest, giving you your raised bed.

If you have enough to spare, it's a good idea to mix a little manure or one of the alternatives, in with the topsoil. This will help open it up, and will improve the water-holding capacity.

8. *Add a generous quantity of manure*

Work down the bed in the same way, filling in the final trench with the soil you dug out of the first.

As you are digging, make sure you get rid of any weeds. Annuals can simply be skimmed off the top with a spade and put in the bottom of the trench. Perennial weeds must be pulled out completely, and put on the bonfire.

Once you have finished digging, remember the golden rule. You should not set a foot on the bed from now until the end of the season when it is dug over again.

If you dig the bed in the autumn or winter there is no need to break the soil down to a fine tilth at that stage. The winter frosts and rains will do that for you.

In the spring all that will then remain to be done, will be to scatter on the surface of the soil the appropriate amount of fertiliser for each crop, and rake it down to a fine tilth.

The second year

The following year, there will be no need to double-dig the bed again. Single digging just the top spit of soil will be

9. *Use the soil from the next trench to fill the first*

10. *Place the manure in a heap behind you*

11. *Scrape the manure forwards to fill the trench*

12. *Cover with soil from the next trench*

sufficient. And when you do come to do it, believe me, you'll find it a great pleasure. Because the soil has not been compacted, the spade will go through it like a knife through butter.

This time the first trench need only be about a spade's width. Instead of barrowing the soil to the end of the plot, simply throw it behind you. You should be able to dig the bed level and, when you get to the final trench, if you don't have enough soil to fill it, scrape a little off the paths between the beds.

The manure again goes in the bottom of the trench but there is no necessity to break up the subsoil, or to mix extra manure into the top (10, 11 & 12).

Sowing and planting

Before sowing or planting in the spring, the first job is to test the soil for lime. Lime-test kits are very cheap and easy to use and will tell you exactly how much lime to apply if your soil is acid. Constant applications of organic matter, especially farmyard manure, are likely to make the soil rather acid, and it is important to correct this with a dressing of garden lime. The one exception to this rule is the area that is to grow potatoes. These prefer a slightly acid soil, and will rarely need liming.

Don't apply the lime at the same time as the manure. This tends to release ammonia, and valuable nitrogen will be lost.

If quality vegetables are to be grown it is essential to provide them with enough food. This is even more important with a highly intensive system like the deep-bed method. Closely-planted vegetables will remove most of the plant food from the soil, and they will compete with each other just like a pack of hungry dogs. So, it really is important to give them enough for all their needs. However, it can be an even worse mistake to give them too much. That could cause damage to the plants, and won't do your pocket any good either!

In the cultivation details given for each vegetable later in this chapter, I have recommended fertiliser rates. These should be strictly adhered to. Use a general fertiliser for each crop. Standardising on one is much simpler and will save money in the end. I have suggested either Growmore, which is readily available in any garden shop, or preferably Double-Strength Growmore. This is a bit cheaper but it does need to be used with care. In fact, the makers supply a small measuring cup with each pack, and I have found this an ideal way of accurately distributing the granules. Naturally you use half the rate I have recommended for Growmore.

If you use Growmore, it is still a good idea to copy this method with a home-made measure. Use a plastic coffee cup and simply weigh out one ounce of fertiliser on the kitchen scales, put it in the cup and mark a line with a waterproof pen to show where one ounce comes to on the side of the cup. Now do the same thing with two, three and four ounces (13).

When it comes to applying the fertiliser to the bed, simply mark out a square yard (or metre). On a 4ft wide (120 cm. wide) bed it will be 2 ft 3 in. (67 cm.) down the bed and sprinkle on the appropriate amount of fertiliser (17).

Ideally, fertilising should be done a couple of weeks before sowing or planting, so that some of the feed is in solution ready for the plants to use immediately. Rake it lightly into the surface of the soil, and you're ready to go.

Sowing and planting should be done to accurate spacings (18). To make this easier, I have found a planting board an invaluable piece of equipment (16). This is simply a piece of timber 3 in. × 1 in. × 8 ft (7.5 × 2.5 × 240 cm.), marked off at 6 in. (15 cm.) intervals with saw cuts. I have also banged in the appropriate number of nails at each foot, just to make sure I get it right first time.

The essence of the deep-bed method is that plants are grown close together in blocks rather than in rows (15). The elimination of paths between the rows dramatically increases the amount of land available for growing crops.

Some crops, like radishes or early carrots, are sown in wide bands rather than in individual drills, and this will also save a lot of space.

13. *A fertiliser measuring cup*

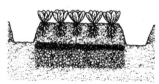

14. *A section through a deep-bed*

Sowing

For crops that are to be sown in rows the technique is very simple. Just place the planting board on edge across the bed, and press it down into the soil, working it backwards and forwards at the same time (23). This will easily produce a drill deep enough for most small seeds.

Larger seeds such as beans and peas are often sown in wider, flat-bottomed drills. Here, the board is placed flat across the bed, and prevented from moving by pushing a couple of canes in the bed immediately behind it. The drill can then be drawn with a draw hoe, using the board as a marker (16). The same method is used for small seeds sown in a strip, but the drill should be made a little shallower.

Make sure, when you sow small seeds in a wide band, that they are sown thinly (20). Bear in mind that most fresh vegetable seed will, if it is sown at the correct depth, give about 80 per cent germination. Too heavy a sowing not only wastes seed, but it tends to produce thin, weak seedlings and increases the work of thinning out. With a bit of practice, you should be able to sow such subjects as radish, carrot and salad onions so that they need no thinning at all.

Bear in mind also, that deep-beds tend to be better

15. *Crops are grown in blocks or wide bands*

16. *Using a planting board*

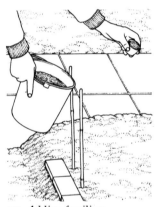

17. *Adding fertiliser*

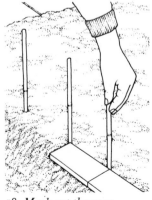

18. *Mark out the rows accurately*

drained than normal. This means that the surface of the soil is likely to be drier than that in the rest of the garden. In dry weather, therefore, provision must be made to ensure that the seeds and the young seedlings have enough water. If the soil is dry, it is a good idea to run a little water into the drill *before* sowing. Don't sow the seeds and then apply water. This tends to form a crust on the top of the soil preventing further water from entering and allowing a build-up of toxic gases beneath it. As the condition of the soil in the beds improves over the years, these precautions become less necessary. The organic matter worked into the soil will rot down to form humus and this will help greatly to retain moisture.

Some plants that are grown at wider spacings can often be 'inter-cropped' with a quick maturing subject. If, for example, you sow a couple of rows of broad beans, there is no reason why a row of radishes should not be sown between the rows. They will be ready to harvest long before the beans have filled their allotted space and the name of our particular game is to use as much of the land available as much of the time as possible. I must say that, although I have tried growing my radishes in a wide band on their own, I have never really found it necessary. If you stick a row in between each widely spaced crop, you'll easily have a good succession without the need to sow them anywhere else.

Planting

Planting crops raised in the greenhouse or in a seed-bed, is always done 'on the square'. This means that, instead of planting in rows with an access path between each row, they are planted in blocks across the bed. As you can imagine, this saves a vast amount of space.

Some crops, such as lettuce, can be planted at a distance that will allow them to just touch when they are mature. But be warned: this does not work for all crops. During the first year in which I tried deep-beds, I planted brussels sprouts a foot apart. They grew very well indeed but, while the plants on the outside rows produced some excellent sprouts, those on the inside were about the size of peas! They need a lot more light and air and a lot less competition if the crop is to be usable.

It should also be remembered that closer planting can be a useful way of controlling the size of the crop. Few small families want cabbages the size of footballs or seven-pound cauliflowers. Closer planting will produce much smaller heads, and of course, many more of them. This avoids waste and makes more efficient use of the land.

Planting in deep-beds is also done with the aid of the planting board – using either a trowel or, because the soil is so soft – your fingers (25). Plant the first row at the recommended distances and set the plants of the second row a little closer, but in between those in the first. This produces a diagonal pattern and again will save space (26).

After planting, give each plant a good drink with a hose or watering can without the rose (27). This will provide sufficient moisture, and settle the soil round the roots.

Planning
After you have spent your first day double-digging, you'll want to sit in front of the fire to rest your aching back. That's the best time to plan the year's sowing and planting. There are two main points to bear in mind.

Firstly, try to work out some sort of rotation. This simply means that you try not to grow the same crop in the same part of the bed two years running. This is mainly to avoid the build-up of pests and diseases. I must say, however, that though the general advice is to sow or plant as far away as you can in the second year from where the crop grew in the first, in a small garden that is pretty pointless. In a small plot, carrot fly *will* find your carrots, even if they are five yards away from where they were the year before. Clubroot *will* spread short distances in the soil and greenfly are going to be everywhere. So, there is no need to get too paranoid about rotations. You will just have to find other ways of controlling pests and diseases. However, in a larger garden it is worthwhile doing it, especially if you have two or three beds to play with.

The second point is, in my opinion, more important. Try to get the overwintering crops planted together at one end of the bed. With a deep-bed, the only real way to do the winter digging is to start at one end and to work right through to the other. There is nothing more annoying than to have to hold up the operation because there is a row of leeks in the way, or because you must wait until you harvest the spring cabbage. Of course it is possible to work around growing crops, but it is nothing like so convenient.

You will have noticed that I have said nothing about leaving a part of the bed unmanured for growing the root crops. Forget it. Though I know that the normal gardening advice is to avoid manured land for root crops because it will make them fork, I have never found this to be so. At Barnsdale, I grew carrots, parsnips and long beet in manured soil, and never had a sign of forking. But the manure *must* be well-rotted. Though I have never tried it myself, I am quite prepared to accept that fresh manure will cause roots to fork. Well-rotted muck or compost doesn't.

Cultivation
While close planting will eventually reduce the weeding problem, it is, if anything, more difficult in the very early

19. *Making a drill with a draw hoe*

20. *Sow in a wide band*

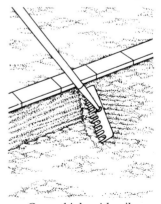

21. *Cover thinly with soil*

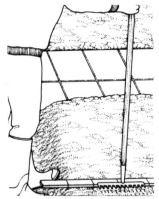

22. *Tamp lightly with the back of a rake*

23. *Marking single rows with the planting board*

24. *Large seeds are sown in stations*

stages. If crops are close, and particularly if they are sown in a band, it is difficult, if not impossible to use a hoe. Though I have managed with a small onion hoe (28) round such crops as lettuce or cabbage in the early stages, weeding is more often than not a hand job. ·

The first essential is to start with clean land. Don't sow or plant if there is any sign of weed seedlings at all. Then, make an inspection of the bed every evening if you can, but certainly once a week, and pull out anything that shouldn't be there. Because the soil is so loose, weeds come up very easily and keeping the beds clean is really quite a pleasure. But you must never, never leave them to get a hold. In the fertile conditions of a deep-bed, weeds will flourish as well as the crop, so it is important to keep on top of them.

Watering

Watering is important, especially if your soil is on the light side. In dry weather it may be necessary to apply extra water, and often even more than you would if you were growing by conventional methods.

The best bet is to get properly geared up for the job right from the start. In dry conditions it's not a bit of good putting on a sprinkle of water from the can. Indeed this will do more harm than good. If you just water the surface of the soil, the roots of your vegetables will come upwards in search of it. Then, when the soil dries out again, they will be even more vulnerable.

So, if you are going to water at all, give the beds a good soaking. Rather than wasting valuable time standing there with the hose, invest in a lawn sprinkler. The best one for the job is the type that consists of a pulsating nozzle mounted on a tall tube (30). This will stand well above most crops, and will water the whole bed evenly.

Pests and diseases

Good garden hygiene is more important on a deep bed than anywhere else. If vegetables are closely planted, any pests and diseases that are allowed to get a hold will have a field day and spread like wildfire.

Regular evening or weekly inspection then, is doubly important. As soon as the first sign of pests or disease appears, it should be attacked vigorously. This does not necessarily mean that the sprayer will be in constant use. Indeed, chemical controls should always be looked upon as a last resort. In the first instance, pick off any diseased leaves and confine them to the bonfire, or put them in a polythene bag in the dustbin. When you see the first caterpillar, pick him off and get rid of him. If you see signs of virus diseases, whip the whole plant out straight away and burn it. That way you can easily stop the problem from spreading.

In the last resort, you will have to use a chemical control, but don't do so until all else has failed.

Quite a lot of pests and diseases can be avoided by keeping the beds clean. As mentioned before, weeds should be removed before they have a chance to spread, and any dead leaves or vegetable debris should be cleaned up regularly. As soon as a crop is cleared, even if you are not going to replant straight away (though you should) remove the crop residues and hoe out any weeds that may be around.

It is often recommended that hardy crops should be left in the ground over the winter. This is a mistake. During the cold, wet weather they are even more vulnerable to attacks by pests and particularly diseases. Parsnips and carrots, for example, can often be attacked by carrot-root fly quite late in the year. It is much better to lift them as soon as they are mature and store them in boxes of sand or peat in the garage. It will also leave your land vacant for the winter digging.

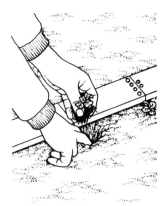
25. *Plant seedlings with your fingers*

Feeding
For most crops, there will be no need to apply further fertiliser after the initial, pre-seeding application. There are a few exceptions. Anything that has overwintered, like Japanese onions or spring cabbage, will benefit from a dressing of nitrogen in the early spring. Plants that make fruit at the same time as they are making growth, like tomatoes, marrows and courgettes, are gross feeders, and should be kept regularly supplied with nutrients. For all these, use a proprietary tomato fertiliser. These are rich in potash and will help to produce an abundance of fruits.

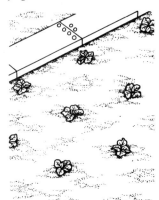
26. *Planting in a diagonal pattern saves space*

Protection
Apart from producing more yield from each square yard, another way to make more efficient use of the land is to extend the season. Deep-beds are ideally suited for growing crops under cloches.

There are plenty of different types available, but ideally, try to find a make of the right size to fit across the bed. If you make the bed 3 ft (1 m.) wide, you'll have no problem at all, but 4 ft (1.2 m.) beds could be a little more tricky. The best solution I found was a large field frame called the 'Melbourne Frame'. This consists of a metal framework in the shape of a tent, with a tailored skin of PVC stretched over it. They are made in various sizes, but the 5 ft (1.5 m.) wide one is ideal for the system. This stretches right over the bed, is light and easy to move on your own, and is equipped with small flaps to let in air and water. They are a bit expensive but the handyman should be able to make something similar in wood.

Use cloches to cover the earliest crops from about the end of January or February (depending on how far north you

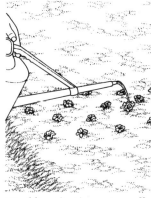
27. *After planting water well*

28. *Weeding with an onion hoe*

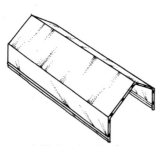

29. *A Melbourne Frame*

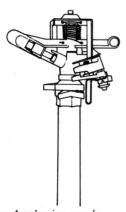

30. *A pulsating nozzle irrigator*

live), and to protect such crops as tomatoes at the end of the season.

To make the best use of cloches, they should be used in succession over a variety of crops.

Start during January or February, depending on where you live, with such hardy crops as broad beans and early peas. Once they are established and on their way, the cloches should be removed and placed over the next stretch of bed for a week or so to warm the soil. Then sow early salads like beetroot, carrots, lettuce and radish.

Make sure when you choose your seed, that the variety is one specifically bred for this type of cultivation. In our trials, I found for example, that the early lettuce Tom Thumb did extremely well, and was several weeks in advance of those sown outside. Under exactly the same conditions, Avoncrisp was much less advanced, only beating those outside by a week or so.

In April or May, the cloches are again moved to cover early-planted marrows, courgettes, melons, peppers, bush tomatoes, cucumbers or sweet corn. Though they can be removed from most of these crops by early to mid-June it is best to keep the more tender peppers, aubergines and melons covered. Make sure though, that pollinating insects can get at the flowers.

At the end of the season, when the weather begins to turn cold and wet, the cloches will again come into use, just to finish off those tender crops that have not quite finished ripening all their fruit.

During the winter, I discovered a novel but extremely useful job for my cloches. Once all the crops were harvested, I covered the bare soil with Melbourne frames (29). They kept the weather off the bed so that, even when he rest of the land was ankle-deep in snow, I was able to get on with the winter cultivations. Particularly in the north of the country, this could be a great advantage, keeping the programme well ahead of normal schedules. If you are going to do this though, don't forget to also cover the muck or compost heap with a sheet of polythene. It's not a good idea to fork frozen material into the bottom of the trenches.

Crop Details

Beetroot
Start the year by sowing an early crop of baby-beet, harvesting them when they are about the size of a golf ball. The earliest sowings can be made in February, sowing in a band with about 2 in. (5 cm.) between seeds. The best varieties are Avonearly or Boltardy.

Before sowing, apply Growmore at 4 oz per sq. yd (120 gm per sq. m.) and rake it in to the surface of the soil. Cover with about ½ in. (13 mm.) of soil and protect the earliest sowings with cloches.

Later sowings can be made outside, starting in early April, using the same varieties and fertiliser rate. Sow this crop in a band in the same way and at the same distance, but thin out when the roots are about the size of a golf ball, leaving some roots to grow bigger (31). This will give a continued harvest, with the largest roots being harvested when they are a little smaller than a cricket ball.

Make further sowings in May, June and July. The final sowing can be lifted in the autumn and the roots stored in sand or peat in a frost-free spot, for use in the winter.

Beetroot are an excellent subject for multiple seeding (see page 36).

31. Thin beetroot selectively

Broad Beans

Though broad beans can be sown in the autumn and overwintered, I try to avoid cluttering the beds and impeding cultivations. They will mature as early from a January or February sowing under cloches.

Certainly for the first sowing, choose a dwarf variety like The Sutton or Bonny Lad. They will not get knocked about in rough weather and are easier to cover with cloches.

Before sowing, rake in a dressing of Growmore at 3 oz per sq. yd (90 gm per sq. m.). Put the seeds in with a trowel, setting them 3 in. (7·5 cm.) deep and 9 in. (23 cm.) apart, in a double row with 9 in. (23 cm.) between the rows (24).

These varieties should not need staking, but in exposed gardens it is a good idea to put a couple of canes at each end of the double row with a string around the plants (32).

If you are a broad bean enthusiast, further sowings can be made in the open ground from February to the middle of April. These are done in exactly the same way as the earlier sowings, but since the crop need not be covered with cloches, taller, more prolific varieties can be used. Imperial Green Windsor and Hysor are good varieties.

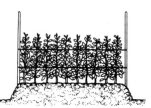

32. Support broad beans with canes

Brussels Sprouts

Brussels must have a fair amount of space if they are to produce sprouts of a usable size. Sow in a seed-bed or in a single row across the deep-bed during March. Sow thinly to avoid thinning out, and cover the seeds with about ½ in. (13 mm.) of soil.

When choosing varieties, try to aim for a succession of maturity. I would suggest Peer Gynt for the earliest crop, followed by Citadel and then Rampart to take cropping through to February or March.

The plants should be ready for their final positions by May or June. Before planting, rake in Growmore at 4 oz per sq. yd (120 gm per sq. m.). The general advice for brussels sprouts is to plant in really firm soil, but I have found no deterioration of the crop when they are planted in the much looser conditions of the deep-bed. Plant in blocks with 2 ft (60 cm.) between plants. At this spacing, the sprouts in the centre of the bed will be a little smaller than those on the outside, but they will be of an acceptable size, and certainly ideal for freezing.

Make sure the plants never go dry, and give them another feed of Growmore at 4 oz per sq. yd (120 gm per sq. m.) during July. Since there is more space between these plants than most, weeds may spring up in between them in the early stages. They are, however, wide enough to allow the use of a hoe.

Cabbage

It is possible to arrange for a succession of cabbage right through the year. In the summer, however, when there is a plentiful supply of more exotic vegetables, you may well decide to give them a rest. It may seem ungrateful but when there are beans, courgettes, fresh peas and the like, I certainly have no room for the humble cabbage.

Cabbage will respond well to being planted closer to control its size. If you want a really large head, plant them further apart, but if your family is small, you will reduce waste, and make more from the land available by closer planting.

Spring Cabbage

Sow in a seed-bed or a single deep-bed row in July in the north and August in the south using varieties April or Avoncrest. The plants will be ready for their final positions in September or October. Remember that this is one of the crops that will overwinter, so they are best planted at one end of the bed.

33. *Harvest alternate spring cabbage*

Before planting, rake in a dressing of Growmore at 4 oz per sq. yd (120 gm per sq. m.).

Spring cabbage can be harvested as greens and later as hearted heads. To make the best use of the land, plant closely together and remove every other plant as greens, allowing the remainder to heart up later (33). Plant in blocks with 1 ft (30 cm.) between the rows and 4 in. (10 cm.) between plants. Make sure that you take precautions against cabbage root fly. In the close environment of a deep-bed, you can be almost sure that they will attack most of the cabbage family at some time. For control methods see pages 54–55.

In the early spring, again apply a dressing of Growmore at 4 oz per sq. yd (120 gm per sq. m.).

Summer Cabbage

The earliest crops of summer cabbage come from plants sown in the greenhouse or cold-frame in January. The first sowings outside are made in a seed-bed in March. For a succession, sow another batch in April and another in May. For the earliest crops use Hispi or Greyhound. For autumn maturing, I was very impressed with Minicole.

Apply Growmore at 4 oz per sq. yd (120 gm per sq. m.) before planting, and set the plants in blocks from 1 ft (30 cm.) to 18 in. (45 cm.) apart depending on the size of head you require. When the plants are well established, give them another feed of Growmore at the same rate.

Winter Cabbage

During the winter, the cabbage once again becomes king of the jungle. There are less other crops available, so it is a truly invaluable crop.

Again, sow the seeds thinly in a seed-bed or a single row in the deep-bed. Use hardy varieties like Celtic or, for a smaller head, the new Aquarius. Sowing takes place in late April/May, and the plants are set in their final positions in June or July. Again, put them at one end of the bed.

Before planting, apply Growmore at 4 oz per sq. yd (120 gm per sq. m.), and set the plants in a block with 15–18 in. (38–45 cm.) between plants. In September, apply another dressing of Growmore at the same rate as before.

Chinese Cabbage

Known, for some incomprehensible reason as 'Chinese Leaves' in the supermarket, this is a relative newcomer to this country. They look like a cross between a cos lettuce and a cabbage and are delicious in salads or better still stir-fried.

They are grown in much the same way as lettuce but, since they are liable to bolt, especially in dry weather, they are not normally sown until mid-May through to July or August. They like a rich soil that will hold plenty of water, so they do particularly well on deep-beds, especially if a little organic matter is worked into the surface.

Normally it is recommended that the plants should not be transplanted but I have found that there is no problem with bolting, provided the seedlings are moved when they are still very small, and they are given plenty of water both before and after transplanting. For earlier crops, sow in the greenhouse in peat blocks as early as May for outside planting or during April for growing under cloches. For early sowings use the variety Nagaoka, and for later use I would recommend Pe-Tsai.

If you can make sure that plants are small when they are transplanted, sow outside in a single row and transplant in blocks with 10 in. (25 cm.) between plants.

If you are at all worried about catching the seedlings at the right stage, or your soil is on the dry side, sow thinly in rows 10 in. (25 cm.) apart and thin the plants to 10 in. (25 cm.) apart.

Before planting, apply Growmore at 4 oz per sq. yd (120 gm per sq. m.) and make sure that the plants never go without water.

One word of warning. Chinese cabbage may not stand in the ground for long periods, particularly in dry weather, so it is better to plant little and often to avoid wastage.

Capsicum

Sweet peppers, whatever the seedsmen may tell you, are not that successful outside without some protection. Under cloches, they work well, and produce a useful crop. The plants must be raised in a heated greenhouse, or bought in at the right time. Frankly, I have found this difficult in most years and impossible in others. You may manage them on a bright, warm windowsill if you are blessed with green fingers but no greenhouse.

Sow the seeds in March or April (34) choosing either Canape or Early Prolific, both of which I have found to do well under cloches. Plant out in late May, after having warmed the soil by covering for at least a fortnight.

Before planting, apply a tomato base fertiliser. There are plenty of proprietary brands, and they should be applied according to the manufacturer's instructions.

Plant in double rows 18 in. (45 cm.) apart with 15 in. (38 cm.) between the plants.

Make sure the plants never go short of water, and feed them once a fortnight with a proprietary tomato fertiliser once the first fruits show.

When the plants reach about 6 in. (15 cm.) high, pinch out the growing point to make them bushy. Though it is always difficult to bring oneself to do it, the first few flowers should be removed, and only about six or eight fruits allowed to mature on each plant.

34. *Sow capsicum in seed trays*

A second planting can be made in late June, though in the north the season may be too short for this.

The fruits are ready for picking when they reach a little less than fist size (the large fruits you see in the shops are grown in heated greenhouses). If you prefer a rather more tangy flavour, leave the fruits to turn red.

Carrots

The earliest carrots can be sown under cloches in January or February to give the first crop of delicious, tender little roots. Again, it is important to choose a forcing variety, and I have found Amsterdam Forcing to be about the best.

Before sowing, dress the soil with Growmore at 1 oz per sq. yd (30 gm per sq. m.), and place the cloches in position a couple of weeks before sowing to warm up the soil.

Sow in a wide band as thinly as is necessary to avoid thinning, and about ½ in. (13 mm.) deep. The first roots can be harvested when they are little thicker than a pencil, selecting them carefully so as to give the remainder a chance to grow.

After this initial sowing, there is no need for cloche cover. From March onwards, sow every month until July, using a maincrop variety like Chantenay Red Cored, Jurawot or Autumn King. The final sowing is for storage for the winter and should be thinned to leave the roots about 4 in. (10 cm.) apart. These are lifted in the autumn and stored in boxes of sand or peat (35).

Take care with the later sowings, to guard against carrot root fly (see pages 55–56).

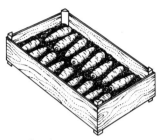

35. *Storing carrots in peat*

Cauliflower

One of my greatest successes in the trials at Barnsdale was with mini-cauliflowers. This is a method of producing small heads, just about big enough for one meal. However, since this is a specialised method, I have described it in more detail later. It is a good example of the way the eventual size of many vegetables can be controlled by spacing. The spacings recommended are for larger heads.

Summer Cauliflower

The earliest crops come from a sowing made in the heated greenhouse in January or February. These will mature from late May. If you have no heat in the greenhouse, you can still have cauliflower at the same time by sowing winter and spring varieties and overwintering them.

Choose an early variety like Alpha Polaris, and sow the seed in boxes of soil-less compost. Transplant them to give about 35 plants per seed tray, and harden them off in a cold frame before planting out in March. Before transplanting check each seedling to make sure it has a growing point. 'Blind' seedlings with just two seed leaves will not grow.

It is important not to allow plants in boxes to become checked through lack of water. This could result in the curds becoming stunted. The secret of good cauliflowers is to keep them growing steadily throughout their lives.

Before planting, apply Growmore at 4 oz per sq. yd (120 gm per sq. m.) and rake it into the surface.

Plant in a block 18–20 in. (45–50 cm.) apart, and water well afterwards.

When the plants are well established and growing away, they will benefit from another dressing of Growmore at the same rate.

Bear in mind that summer cauliflowers will not stand too long without deterioration of quality, so sow only as many as you require at a time and do so at regular intervals.

The second sowing should be in a seed-bed or single row of the deep-bed in March, followed by further sowings once a month until May (36). Plant them out before they get too big, watering the row well before lifting. Planting and

36. *Sow cauliflower seeds in a seed-bed*

fertilising are the same as recommended for those raised in the greenhouse.

Make sure that the plants never go short of water, and take precautions against cabbage root fly (see pages 54–55), since cauliflowers are most prone to attack out of all the cabbage family.

Autumn Cauliflower

The Australian varieties of autumn cauliflower are becoming popular and deservedly so. They have done well for me in deep-beds. Maintain a succession by choosing varieties Bondi, South Pacific and Canberra. Sow in a seed-bed or single row in April and plant out in the same way as summer cauliflower only 2 ft (60 cm.) apart.

Winter Cauliflower

A mid-April to mid-May sowing is early enough for winter varieties which will be ready for cutting from January to June if required. Make sure, if you live in the north, that you choose only the hardiest varieties. Most Walcheren Winter varieties should be hardy enough except in the coldest parts of the country. It is a good idea to break a few leaves over the developing curds to give added protection.

Celery

New varieties of self-blanching celery are a great improvement on the tough, stringy types we used to have to pick out of our teeth before. It is not, in my opinion, worth growing blanched celery in deep-beds since the soil preparation would be the same in the conventional plot. However, because of the high organic matter content of deep-beds, self-blanching types do very well.

The best variety for this sort of culture is Lathom Self-blanching.

If you want celery early in the year (and why not after all?) the plants must be started off in a heated greenhouse. Sow from early February in seed trays, subsequently transplanting to give 35 plants per tray. Plant out under cloches in April, setting the plants in a block 9 in. (23 cm.) apart. Before planting out, apply a dressing of Growmore at 4 oz per sq. yd (120 gm per sq. m.), and rake it into the surface.

Make sure that the plants never go short of water or the stems will become stringy. At that spacing they will not need earthing-up since the plants will shade each other. The sticks on the outside of the bed may be a little greener than those on the inside, but they will still be acceptable.

Further sowings can be made for later maturity. It will take roughly 22 weeks from sowing to maturity. Later sowings will not need the protection of cloches.

If at the end of the year there are still some plants left to harvest, protect them from frost with cloches.

Cucumber
All the cucumber family do well in deep-beds because of the high content of organic matter. However, cucumbers take up a fair amount of room so you should think long and hard before deciding to allot them valuable space. They do not produce a very large yield, so in small gardens it is perhaps better to leave them alone.

The first sowings take place in late March or early April in the heated greenhouse. Sow a couple of seeds in pots of soil-less compost, keeping the germinated seedlings near to the glass until early May. They can then be transferred to the deep-bed 2 ft (60 cm.) apart, and covered with cloches. The cover should be put over the soil a fortnight before planting to warm it up. Also before planting, rake in a proprietary tomato base fertiliser and, once the first fruits set, give them a liquid tomato feed every fortnight. Make sure that the plants never go without water.

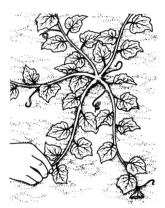

37. *Pinch out the growing points to keep cucumbers in check*

As soon as the plants start to stray from their allotted space, pinch out the growing points to keep them in check (37).

A later crop can be grown without protection, but this should not be planted out until at least the first week in June.

If you have no greenhouse, it is perfectly possible to raise cucumbers by sowing direct in the soil, either under cloches or in the open. Under cloches, sow two seeds at each 'station', with 2 ft (60 cm.) between stations in early May. When the seedlings germinate, remove the weakest and then grow them on as recommended.

Remember that ridge, or outdoor cucumbers *do* need to be pollinated, unlike their hothouse cousins. So, don't make the mistake of removing the male flowers.

French Beans
Another ideal deep-bed crop. They love the warmer soil achieved by raising the beds but care must be taken, especially in the early stages after planting, to ensure that they have adequate supplies of water.

Plants can be raised in the greenhouse and planted under cloches for the earliest crop. Sow two seeds to a 3 in. (7.5 cm.) pot in March and after germination remove the weakest.

Before planting out apply Growmore at 4 oz per sq. yd (120 gm per sq. m.) and cover the soil with the cloches for a couple of weeks to warm it up. French beans hate cold feet, so this is most important.

Plant out in blocks 18 in. (45 cm.) apart, and water well afterwards.

From the end of April onwards the seeds can be sown direct in the beds, at the same spacings, setting two seeds per station, 2 in. (5 cm.) deep. I have found it unnecessary to

38. *Use a hoe handle to plant leeks*

thin if two plants germinate. They will still produce the same amount of beans.

Repeat sowings at monthly intervals will produce a succession of beans until October. The final sowings can again be covered with cloches to extend the picking season.

Leeks

An excellent crop for the deep-bed and a good subject for multiple seeding (see page 37).

The plants are raised either in the greenhouse from a February sowing, or in a seed-bed or single row of the deep-bed from a March sowing. Recommended varieties are Catalina and Argenta.

Plant when the seedlings are about 6 in. (15 cm.) high, after raking in a dressing of Growmore at 4 oz per sq. yd (120 gm per sq. m.).

Plant in blocks with 6 in (15 cm.) between plants. Use either a long dibber or a hoe handle to make the holes (38). The soil is very soft and there is no reason why the dibber should not be pushed in as far as it will go. When the plants are dropped into the holes, they will completely disappear, but will soon grow out again.

Trim the roots and the tops by about a third before planting, and then simply pour a little water down the hole to wash the soil over the roots. With such deep planting holes, the length of blanched stem is greatly increased and there is no need for earthing up – a difficult operation on a deep-bed.

Once the plants are established, they should be given a second dressing of Growmore at 2 oz per sq. yd (60 gm per sq. m.).

If at the end of the year the plants are in the way of winter digging, lift them and set them in bundles in a corner with the roots and blanched part of the stem covered with soil.

Lettuce

It is possible to achieve a great saving of space with lettuce, since they can be grown in a block at a spacing that will allow them to touch on maturity. It should also be possible, with the aid of cloches, to have fresh lettuce right through from May to November. Lettuce is also a good candidate for the multiple seeding technique, growing four plants in a peat block. Leaf lettuce, grown on the cut-and-come-again system can also be done in the deep-bed, and this is explained fully on pages 45–46.

Start the year by sowing an early variety in the greenhouse in February. Tom Thumb is ideal, producing small, crisp hearts very quickly. They can be planted out in the deep-bed in March, after first warming the soil with cloches. Before planting, rake in Growmore at 4 oz per sq. yd (120 gm per sq. m.).

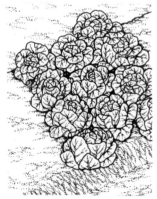

39. *Plant the lettuce close together in the deep-bed*

Set the plants out in a block about 6 in. (15 cm.) apart, and water them in afterwards.

In the middle of February, seed can be sown under cloches, using the variety Avoncrisp. Sow these in a single row for thinning and transplanting later. These must be set out again in a block but, since they produce bigger heads, about 8 in. (20 cm.) apart. The transplanted block will mature just a little later than the thinned row.

Successional sowings of the same variety should be made at fortnightly intervals, in the same way, up until July. Then it is better to revert to Avondefiance, because it is resistant to lettuce mildew, which is prevalent at the end of the year. The late crops can be covered with cloches to prolong the season.

Marrow and Courgettes

On the deep-bed, it is obviously sensible to choose bush, rather than trailing varieties of marrow, since they take up less room and are easier to control. Long Green Bush is a good variety for marrows, and for courgettes, which should be cut much smaller there is still nothing to beat Zucchini.

They are grown in exactly the same way as cucumbers (page 23), except that there is no need to pinch out the growing points.

Melons

Melons are also grown like cucumbers, though they need to be covered with cloches throughout their lives in most parts of the country. Make sure that pollinating insects are allowed into the cloches, and keep the plants under control by pinching. The variety Sweetheart is excellent.

Onion

Salad onions can be grown in wide bands across the bed from a first sowing in February under cloches. The variety White Lisbon is still the best traditional variety, though the new Japanese variety Kincho, which produces much bigger stems is well worth a try.

Before sowing all onions, rake in Growmore at 4 oz per sq. yd (120 gm per sq. m.).

Sow salad onions sparingly to avoid thinning and make sure they have adequate water supplies throughout. Like radishes, the secret of success is to grow them fast.

Make the second sowing in March outside in the same way and continue at monthly intervals until September. The final crop can again be covered with cloches to extend the season.

Maincrop bulb onions can be raised from seed sown in the greenhouse in January, sown outside during March, or planted as sets in February or March. I prefer to raise them from seed in the greenhouse. The seed is sown thinly in

40. *Planting greenhouse-raised onion seedlings*

trays and transplanted 40 to a tray as soon as the plants are large enough to handle. They should be put in the cold-frame about early March to harden them off before planting out towards the end of the month. Plant in a block with 6 in. (15 cm.) between plants. Weeding can be a problem with closely planted onions and it is essential to keep the crop clean. There are now very effective pre-emergence weedkillers that will do the job for you with only two or perhaps three applications.

If you have no greenhouse, sow outside during March in rows 6 in. (15 cm.) apart. Thin as soon as the plants are large enough, to leave them spaced 6 in. (15 cm.) square.

Sets are small onion bulbs. These are planted in February or March, again at 6 in. (15 cm.) spacings. In the soft soil of the deep-bed, they can simply be pushed into the ground, but it is worth checking afterwards that the birds have not pulled them out again.

Japanese onions can be grown at the same spacings. These are described in more detail on pages 59–62.

Parsnip

Despite the manure in the deep-bed parsnips will grow extremely well without forking. Indeed, the loose soil enables them to reach right down to the bottom of the bed, producing some really long roots.

Before sowing, rake in Growmore at 3 oz per sq. yd (90 gm per sq. m.).

If there is any evidence from previous crops of canker in the soil use a resistant variety. Avonresister is ideal. However, the roots of this are smaller than Improved Hollow Crown, which is preferable in clean soil.

41. *Sow parsnip seeds in stations*

Sow the seed in 'stations' with three seeds per station, 6 in. (15 cm.) apart in blocks during February or March (41). It takes a long time to germinate, so don't despair for six to eight weeks.

After the seedlings emerge, thin them to leave one plant per station. After that there is little to do except to keep them weed-free. Protect them against carrot fly and lift them in the autumn and store them in boxes of sand or peat.

Potatoes

Early potatoes are a good subject for deep-beds, though they need to be grown a little differently. There is little point in growing maincrop potatoes if space is the primary problem. You will never grow them as cheaply as the farmer can, and they will be no better. New potatoes dug fresh from the garden and eaten straight away are delicious so even though they take up a fair amount of room, that unique experience in the early summer makes them well worthwhile.

It is difficult to recommend a variety since flavour seems to vary so much in different districts. I have found Maris

Bard, which is a very early and prolific variety to be a favourite on my soil.

Ideally, get hold of some large tubers and start them off in the greenhouse or on the kitchen windowsill in February, placing them in a light, fairly warm spot to sprout. Have a look at the tubers, and sort out which end has the most eyes. They should be set upright in boxes with this end upwards. Don't put them in the dark as some gardeners do. This will give long, pale sprouts that make a weak start. What you need are short, stubby, green sprouts when the tubers are planted. This process of sprouting before planting is important and should not be neglected. It has been found to increase the weight and earliness of the crop considerably.

Before planting, apply a dressing of Growmore at 4 oz per sq. yd (120 gm per sq. m.). The tubers can go in the ground in March. When they show through, keep a weather eye open for frost. If it threatens, cover the crop with cloches, or with slitted polythene. In fact, they can be grown under slitted polythene right from the start and this method is fully explained from pages 69 to 70. Before planting, count the number of sprouts on the tubers and rub off all but four.

Plant with a trowel about 4 in. (10 cm.) deep and 1 ft (30 cm.) apart in a block (42). On a deep-bed, planted this way, it is virtually impossible to earth up, but provided they are planted as described, this should not be necessary.

42. Plant potato tubers with a trowel

If some tubers do have green patches on them when they are lifted, cut them out before eating them. The green parts are poisonous and can cause stomach pains.

When the shoots show through make sure that they have plenty of water. Except in very wet weather, it is always worth watering by hand, since it not only increases the total weight of the crop, but will also help prevent scab.

When the shoots are about 6 in. (15 cm.) high, and before they cover the ground, give them another feed of Growmore at the same rate.

Small tubers should be ready at some time during June. Scrape away a little soil from round the base of the plants and have a look. If they are big enough to eat, take just what you need for one meal, and replace the soil. That way, the rest of the tubers will keep growing and will always have that 'harvest-fresh' flavour.

If you wish to save some seed for planting next year, select enough tubers about the size of a hen's egg, and store them in a sack or open paper bag, but not a polythene bag. It is much, much better to start fresh each year with certified seed that you *know* will be free from virus infection.

Radish
The earliest radish should be sown thinly in a band under cloches in February. After that, I always use radish to fill the

space between rows of slower maturing crops or in any vacant space waiting for the next crop. I have found that this will generally maintain a succession throughout the year.

Remember that it is much better to sow little and often as most varieties become woody if left in the ground for any length of time.

There are many excellent varieties about these days, but I'm afraid to say that my own favourite still remains the good old-fashioned French Breakfast. Try a few others though, to see which you prefer.

If you are sowing them between other crops, they will have to make do with the fertiliser you have applied for the main crop. If you are growing them specifically, rather than as an inter-crop, give them a feed of Growmore at 1 oz per sq. yd (30 gm per sq. m.) before sowing, and sow at fortnightly intervals.

Shallot

Harvested before onions, shallots are a useful crop to fill the gap between the stored and the new crop. They are also ideal for pickling.

They are grown from bulbs harvested from last year's crop rather than from seed. Good varieties are Dutch Yellow and Dutch Red. Hative de Niort will give large bulbs, and a heavy crop, but is not a good keeper. Before planting apply Growmore at 4 oz per sq. yd (120 gm per sq. m.).

Set the bulbs in blocks with 6 in. (15 cm.) between them. In the soft soil of the deep bed, they can be pressed in so that the tops are just showing (43). Check the following day to ensure that birds have not pulled them out again.

There is little to do until harvesting time in June except to keep the plants weed-free. Lift them in June, dry them, clean off dirt and excess skin and store them in nets in a frost-free shed. Remember to save enough bulbs for use as seed next year.

43. *Press in shallots so that tops just show*

Spinach

Under normal circumstances, spinach is not the easiest of crops to grow. In the summer, if the weather is hot and dry it tends to run to seed, while winter varieties suffer in cold, wet weather.

On the deep-bed, it is possible to provide them with ideal conditions. Because of the high organic matter content, they are less likely to run short of water, and the good drainage makes for warmer soil in the winter. If you have given it up as a bad job already, have another go on a deep-bed.

For summer sowing I like Long Standing Round or the newer Norvak. Greenmarket has always done well for me in the winter.

Before sowing, rake in a dressing of Growmore at 4 oz per sq. yd (120 gm per sq. m.). The first sowings of the summer varieties can be made during February and covered with cloches. At the beginning of March they can be sown in the open ground, and from then on at monthly intervals until July, when the winter varieties take over. Sow in a block in 'stations' with three seeds per station, 6 in. (15 cm.) apart. There is really no need to thin the plants since, even if three seedlings grow, they will make the same size as one plant.

During hot, dry weather it is worth watering by hand, just to make sure the plants don't run to seed.

Sow the winter varieties in the same way. In many parts of the country, it will pay to cover the plants with cloches from October onwards.

Pick over the plants regularly, taking a few larger leaves from each, rather than stripping one or two bare (44).

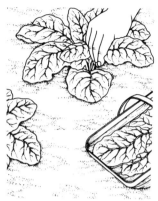

44. *Harvest spinach leaves sparingly*

Swedes

Many people abhor swedes as simply cattle feed. Others, myself included, remember the ghastly taste from school dinners. But, if you haven't tried the new varieties, do so. They are much improved and have certainly become a firm favourite of mine. I have had great success with the new variety Marion which is also resistant to club-root and mildew.

Before sowing, rake in a dressing of Growmore at 3 oz per sq. yd (90 gm per sq. m.). Sowing should not take place until May in the south and June in the north. This later sowing helps to avoid attacks by mildew.

Sow in stations in a block with 1 ft (30 cm.) between stations. There will be no need for more than two seeds per station, since germination is always very good. When the seedlings are large enough to handle, thin them to leave the strongest.

Lift the roots in October or November and store them in boxes of sand or peat.

Sweet Corn

To be quite sure that sweet corn ripens before the end of the year, the plants need to be raised in the greenhouse. It is possible to sow outside under cloches in the south of the country but even so this may be a bit risky.

Sow two seeds to a pot of soil-less compost in gentle heat in April and thin later to leave one seedling. After hardening off in the cold frame, they will be ready for planting out in June.

There are many good, new varieties that are worth a try. I have found Earliking to be consistently good and early to ripen.

Before planting, rake in a dressing of Growmore at 4 oz per sq. yd (120 gm per sq. m.), and plant in blocks 18 in. (45 cm.) apart.

The cobs are ready to harvest when the tassels at the top

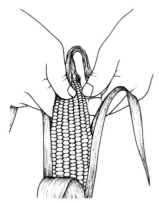

45. *Testing sweet corn for ripeness*

46. *Harden off tomatoes before planting*

turn black. Then open up the leaves covering the cob and squeeze a seed between your thumb nails. If a milky liquid exudes, the cob is ripe (45).

If the liquid is clear, replace the leaves and leave it to ripen a little longer. Remember that, as soon as a cob is removed from the plant, the sugars start to turn to starch, so pick only as you need them, and cook them immediately.

Tomatoes

Bush tomatoes are easy to grow and ideally suited to deep-bed culture. They can in fact be sown outside to give a crop in August or September, and that method is described on page 41. For an earlier crop, plants will have to be raised in the greenhouse.

There are now many varieties of bush tomatoes to choose from. I like Sigmabush, Sleaford Abundance, Alfresco and Sub Arctic Plenty.

Sow in gentle heat in March or early April. Transplant the seedlings to pots and grow them on with plenty of space between plants. They can go out into the cold frame in early May for hardening off before planting in early June (46). Before planting, dress the area with a proprietary tomato base fertiliser according to the manufacturer's instructions.

Plant out in a double row, if you need that many, 20 in. (50 cm.) apart. This close spacing will also tend to give earlier yields.

When the first tiny fruits show, give the plants a feed with a proprietary liquid tomato fertiliser once a fortnight.

When the branches are loaded with fruit, they tend to rest on the soil, so it is worthwhile putting a little straw or peat under them to keep the fruits off the ground.

The crop can be covered with cloches at the end of the season to extend the harvest.

Turnip

The earliest turnips are sown under cloches in February, and harvested when they are about the size of a golf ball.

Use an early variety like Early Snowball, and sow thinly in a wide band. Before sowing rake in a dressing of Growmore at 4 oz per sq. yd (120 gm per sq. m.).

From the end of March, further sowings are made in the same way outside. Thin these selectively, starting when the roots are the size of a golf ball, and allowing the remainder to grow to the size of a cricket ball, or a little smaller. The final sowing should be lifted in October and stored in boxes of sand or peat.

Multiple Seeding

Peat Blocks

Peat blocks have been used for many years by commercial growers with great success. Now they are available to amateur gardeners and appear to have as many, if not more advantages. At Barnsdale, we have been experimenting with plants grown in peat blocks for a couple of years and their range of uses and versatility seem quite exciting.

Of course, soil blocks have been around for many years and some gardeners still use them with varying success. Like soil-based composts, the main disadvantage with soil blocks is that the soil content is likely to be variable. If you can get hold of a good, fibrous loam, preferably derived from stacked turf, they are likely to be successful. But good loam is getting more and more difficult to come by yet there still seems to be a plentiful supply of peat.

Apart from the obvious advantages of availability, peat composts have many points in their favour.

They are light and easy to handle, they can be varied at will to suit a wide range of plants and they vary in quality far less than their soil-based counterparts. This means that they will produce exactly the same results time after time. So once you get used to using them you'll be much more likely to be successful all the time.

But peat-based composts and peat blocks, in particular, *do* take a bit of getting used to. Peat tends to dry out very quickly and, once it does, it can be difficult to wet. Conversely, overwatering can reduce the compost to a waterlogged mass quite unsuitable for good root growth. But if you are prepared to give that little extra care and attention, success is virtually assured.

Peat blocks are made with a special blocking compost. Don't try to use ordinary peat. The blocks may last a few days, but they are bound to fall apart long before the plant roots grow sufficiently to hold them together.

Two manufacturers are now making blocking composts and they also supply a small hand tool for making the blocks. Both are available at most good garden shops. The blocks are quick and easy to make and certainly add to the fun of growing your own.

For the home gardener with a greenhouse there are many advantages. Plants can be raised in peat blocks for planting out later, when they will suffer no root damage at all. Plants grown in seed trays and planted 'bare-rooted' will always suffer a slight check because of the damage to their roots when they are removed from the boxes, but block-grown plants will romp away right from the start.

When the weather or soil conditions are unfavourable for

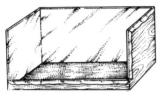

47. *A home-made light trap*

48. *Measure out the compost before mixing*

49. *Mix the compost thoroughly with water until it is evenly wet*

sowing, seeds can be sown in blocks at the right time and under perfect conditions. Then as soon as the soil is all right, you'll have ready-grown plantlets to set out with no consequent delay in harvesting time.

The commercial grower will always get his crop sown at exactly the right time because, of course, his living depends upon it. But gardeners may not find it so convenient. Maybe it will be incumbent upon you to pay a duty visit to Auntie Mabel, or you may be on holiday at the crucial time. No worries – if you can put a little heat on, plants raised in blocks will soon catch up on those sown outside and nothing will be lost.

For gardeners in the north, peat blocks are a positive boon. Take onions for example: in the north, cool springs can lead to late germination and establishment. Since the popular Rijnsburger type onions will not start to bulb until the days are fourteen hours in length – generally during late May – it is essential to have the plants at an advanced stage of maturity at this time if decent-sized bulbs are to be produced. In a cold, late spring, when germination and establishment are delayed, bulbing may not take place until late June or early July, which will not give the plants time to produce good sized bulbs.

If the seeds are sown in peat blocks in January, the plants will be at the right stage of maturity when the days are long enough to initiate bulbing and good crops are assured.

If you have no greenhouse, it is possible to grow reasonable plants on the kitchen windowsill, provided the temperature can be maintained at a minimum of 60°F (15°C) day and night.

Even if this temperature can be maintained, the biggest problem in the kitchen or the front room is lack of light. Even though you may be blessed with a sunny windowsill, there is rarely the same level of light that would be available in the greenhouse.

To overcome this I built myself a mini-light-trap which, while not perfect, produced quite acceptable plants. It cost me only a few pence, so was certainly worth doing.

Simply beg, borrow or steal an orange or apple box from the greengrocer. Knock out one long side to give a three-sided box. The inside of the box is now covered with kitchen foil – the only part of the job that costs any money. A trip down to the carpet shop should bring forth a couple of off-cuts of fibre carpet underfelt. When I asked, they thought I was crazy, but they were only too pleased to give me a couple of square yards for nothing. The underfelt goes in the bottom of the box in place of expensive capillary matting and does as good a job. Set the box on a table facing the window and that's all there is to it (47).

The foil will catch and reflect all the available light and

also prevents water slopping all over the living-room carpet.

The blocks themselves are simple and quick to make. It is fairly important to make the compost wet enough, or they will fall apart quickly. It is better to make it too wet rather than too dry but it is easy to get the water content just right. This is done by mixing the compost and the water in a bowl, measuring out the quantities in a jug or similar container. Use four times as much compost as water and you will get the correct consistency (48 & 49).

Mix the compost thoroughly and then fill the tool, scraping any excess compost from the top with a flat piece of wood. Then put the tool down onto a flat base and press down the plunger to compress the compost and squeeze out any excess water. The finished block can then be pushed out by raising the tool and pushing down the plunger (51).

50. *Fill the blocking tool with the wetted compost*

The blocks can then be placed in a seed tray, but ideally they should go onto an absorbent mat. A piece of capillary matting placed over a sheet of polythene is ideal, or, as suggested before, use a piece of fibre carpet underfelt (53).

It is important when setting out the blocks, to ensure that they do not touch (54). If they do, the roots of the seedlings may spread from block to block and these will have to be broken before planting. That way, there will be considerable check to growth because of root damage and one of the main advantages will be lost.

The blocks can then be sown (52). If you are only after one plant per block, put in a couple of seeds, and thin later to leave the strongest. The multiple seeding technique is explained on pages 34–38.

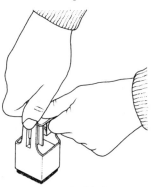

51. *Push out the block on a hard surface*

The blocks can now be covered with a sheet of black polythene but I have found much greater success if a little silver sand is sprinkled over the seeds first (55).

Look at the blocks every day and never let either they or the capillary matting dry out. In the early spring, with heat in the greenhouse, this may mean a daily light wetting with a fine rose on the watering can. Once the seedlings emerge, the polythene should be removed.

When the plants start to grow away, it is even more important to pay particular attention to watering, since they will also be removing water from the blocks.

If daily attention is difficult, it is possible to buy a special capillary mat that is self-watering. This consists of a small trough into which part of the mat is dipped. The water from the trough will spread over the whole mat and is kept topped up with a small header-tank, which should only need attention once or twice a week.

As the seedlings grow, their roots will fill the block, and perform another useful function in holding the block firmly together. If the plants are in the blocks for a long time, as onions would be for example, it is worthwhile giving them a

52. *Multiple seeding peat blocks*

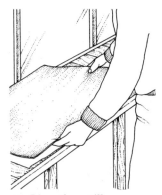

53. *Place the capillary matting over a sheet of polythene*

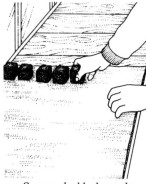

54. *Set out the blocks so that they do not touch*

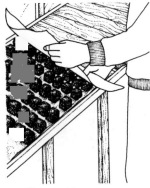

55. *Cover with opaque polythene to prevent evaporation*

feed with liquid general fertiliser after about six weeks.

Once the plant roots emerge from the sides of the blocks, they should be planted out as quickly as possible. If they are left too long, they will root into the matting or into the adjacent blocks and root damage will occur.

Before planting, the blocks must be transferred to seed trays and gradually hardened off in the cold-frame to get them used to the colder outside temperatures.

It has been noticed that wet blocks will transplant well into wet or dry soil, but dry blocks will not establish well even if the soil is wet. It is essential, therefore, to ensure that the blocks get a good soaking before planting.

Once they are planted it is a good practice to water the soil well and to apply another feed of general liquid fertiliser.

Multiple Seeding

The only disadvantage with peat blocks, is that a lot of blocks are required and they are not as cheap as could be desired.

This material disadvantage was felt even more keenly by commercial growers with the result that considerable research has been carried out to see if more than one plant could not be grown in the same block. Thus the technique known as 'multiple seeding' was born.

The method of growing the seedlings is exactly the same as that described for single-seeded blocks, except that more seeds are used per block.

Instead of sowing two seeds and thinning later to leave one plant, several seeds are sown in each block and allowed to grow. The block is then planted out with all the seedlings growing in a clump. At first sight this seems the height of folly. We all know that unthinned plants in a row produce weak specimens which crop very badly indeed.

In fact, provided the blocks are planted at the correct spacings, the plants jostle for space, pushing each other out of the way to find their own room and produce a good crop of perfectly-formed plants. We tried it first of all with onions and found that as the bulbs grew, they pushed against each other until some were growing almost horizontally to the ground. But they still produced perfectly shaped bulbs, and in fact a bigger crop per square yard than those grown conventionally (56).

Most of the work on multiple seeding has been done on onions. We have tried some other crops with great success but there is still a lot of experimenting to do with other vegetables. One failure we had, for example, was with carrots. They simply wound around each other in the ground, and the resultant crop was quite useless.

I have now tried the technique with onions, leeks, beetroot, sweet corn, self-blanching celery, cabbage, lettuce and tomatoes, all with successful results. The failures have been the long root crops like carrots and parsnips, for the reason described.

Onions

It is the custom amongst gardeners who grow large onions for exhibition, to sow them very early – mid-to-late December being considered the optimum time. However, research at the Stockbridge House Experimental Horticultural Station has shown no advantage in sowing this early. They recommend a mid-to-late-January sowing. In view of the greatly increased cost of maintaining adequate temperatures for that extra month, even a small decrease in yield must be considered acceptable. In fact, under normal garden conditions, yields should be about the same.

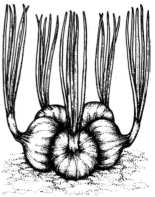

56. *Multiple-seeded onions will still produce perfectly shaped bulbs*

Make up the peat blocks as described, and sow six seeds per block. I have found that the best way to do this is to spread out the seed on a sheet of card and to push them into the small depression in the block with the tip of a penknife (52).

After sowing, cover the seeds with a sprinkle of silver sand. In one trial at Barnsdale I excluded the sand, with the result that establishment was considerably reduced. Some blocks at planting time contained only one or two seedlings, while those covered contained between five and six.

The blocks should then be placed on a piece of capillary matting and covered with black polythene, and the temperature must be maintained at 60°F (15°C). Remove the polythene when the seedlings germinate and ensure that the blocks receive adequate water. Maintain the temperature for a further four weeks, after which it can be dropped to 50°F (10°C). Finally, harden off the plants in a cold-frame before planting out. After the plants have been growing for about six weeks, they will benefit from a feed with a general liquid fertiliser. This can be applied through a watering can fitted with a fine rose.

Before planting, rake the bed down to a fine tilth, at the same time working in Growmore at 4 oz per sq. yd (120 gm per sq. m.).

The blocks after hardening off can be planted during March or April, setting the top of the block level with the soil surface.

Though they can be planted in rows, the best arrangement is to set the blocks out in beds with 1 ft (30 cm.) between them. They are an ideal subject for the deep-bed method of cultivation.

As mentioned before, it is important to ensure that the blocks are given a good soaking before planting and to water them well afterwards.

During the season, there is little more to do except to keep the soil between the plants weed-free. The bulbs will push each other out of the way and though they grow at all sorts of strange angles, will produce perfect bulbs by late July or August.

I did notice at Barnsdale that the multiple-seeded onions were a little later in showing signs of maturity in the foliage than the conventionally sown plants. This could be because the close planting tends to exclude the sun. It is worthwhile, especially in the north, to put a fork underneath the cluster of bulbs to raise it slightly and thus break the roots. This will hasten the withering of the foliage and subsequent ripening of the bulbs. Do *not* as is sometimes recommended, bend the tops over by hand. This could damage the necks and allow disease to enter, thus reducing storage life.

The best variety for me was Hygro and this is also the one recommended by Stockbridge House EHS. It is a well-shaped onion with a good colour and flavour and it has the added advantage of storing well.

Beetroot
Growing early beetroot in peat blocks has one great advantage apart from those already mentioned. As you know, transplanting beetroot seedlings bare-rooted is fraught with dangers unless the seedlings are very small indeed. Often the roots will fork and become useless in the kitchen. In peat blocks this does not happen because there is no disturbance to the root system. So, growing in peat blocks in gentle heat, enables very early crops to be harvested.

The ideal is to grow four or five seedlings per block. Unless you use one of the new 'mono-germ' seeds (that is one where only one seed in the cluster will germinate), there is no necessity to sow more than two seeds per block. Each cluster will contain several seeds, of which at least two are bound to come up. In fact I tried originally sowing only one seed cluster per block. In some cases, this only produced two or three seedlings, so I now sow two. If more than six seedlings emerge, the extras can easily be removed.

Sow in late January in the same way and at the same temperatures recommended for onions. Harden the plants off a little in the cold-frame and then transfer them to beds outside, again planting at 1 ft (30 cm.) apart, in March. Before planting, rake in a dressing of Growmore at 4 oz per sq. yd (120 gm per sq. m.).

It is a good idea to warm up the soil in advance by covering it with cloches for about a fortnight. Replace the cloches after planting.

Harvest the beet when they are no bigger than a golf ball. They may be a little flattened on one side but apart from that they make very good eating indeed. For early growing, use an early maturing variety like Avonearly or Boltardy.

If the multiple-seeding system is to be used for the maincrop sowing (though I see little advantage), grow only three seedlings per block, and harvest when the roots are about the size of a cricket ball, or a little smaller.

Multiple-seeded beet are another excellent subject for deep-bed cultivation.

Leeks

Use exactly the same method for leeks as recommended for onions. Sow six seeds per block during late January or early February at 60°F (15°C). Harden off and plant out in April 1 ft (30 cm.) square.

Generally leeks are planted in a dibbed hole but this is unnecessary for this method. Closely planted like this, they tend to blanch each other and I found that the extra number of plants per square yard, more than made up for the slightly shorter blanched stem.

At Barnsdale, the plants stood a fairly hard winter with no ill effects, and were still usable during March the following year.

The variety I used was Catalina. Again, this is a good subject for deep-beds.

Lettuce

Another vegetable that is only worth multiple seeding for the very early crop grown under cloches.

Sow in the heated greenhouse at 60°F (15°C) in early February, putting three seeds to each block. Plant them out under cloches in March, having warmed the soil first by setting out the cloches a fortnight earlier.

Before planting rake in Growmore at 4 oz per sq. yd (120 gm per sq. m.). The smaller varieties, like Tom Thumb can be planted 9 in. (23 cm.) square, but larger varieties like Avoncrisp must go a little wider at 1 ft (30 cm.) square.

Cabbage

Do not sow cabbage as thickly as other crops. The optimum is two plants per block, and since most of the seeds will germinate, there is no need to sow more than two seeds.

Sow early varieties in the greenhouse in gentle heat at 50°F (10°C) in January or February and plant out under cloches in March.

Before planting rake in Growmore at 4 oz per sq. yd (120 gm per sq. m.), setting the plants 18 in. (45 cm.) apart. This will give heads of average size, generally big enough for the small family. Wider spacing will give bigger heads but less crop per square yard.

The cloches can be removed in May, or when the cabbages outgrow them.

The best varieties for early summer crops are Hispi or Derby Day.

Sweet Corn

It can be somewhat difficult to time tender crops when growing them in peat blocks. It is important to get the plants as big as possible for planting out, but they should not be too big or the roots will grow out of the blocks and into each other or the capillary matting. This will result in root damage and should certainly be avoided in sweet corn, which hates disturbance.

I found that the best time to sow at Barnsdale was in mid-April, but this could well be advanced in the south of the country and it could be prudent to wait until the last week in April in the north. If the plants begin to outgrow the blocks, it is better to plant out under cloches than to delay until root damage is inevitable.

Sow three seeds per block in a temperature of 60°F (15°C). Plant out in late May or early June, or a little earlier if you intend to use cloches.

It is important to plant in blocks rather than in rows to ensure pollination setting the plants 2 ft (60 cm.) apart. Rake in a dressing of Growmore at 4 oz per sq. yd (120 gm per sq. m.) before planting.

Many varieties are available and most have something to recommend them. I found Earliking to be the most successful at Barnsdale.

Celery

Celery is generally considered a winter crop, but there is no reason why self-blanching varieties should not be grown for use in the summer.

Sow in February, putting three or four seeds per block. Celery seed is quite small, so you'll need a steady hand for this job. If you find that you have sown more when they germinate, thin them to leave three plants per block.

The temperature should be maintained at 60°F (15°C) until four weeks after germination when it can be dropped to 50°F (10°C).

Before planting out, warm the soil with cloches and rake in a dressing of Growmore at 4 oz per sq. yd (120 gm per sq. m.). Plant in April or early May, setting the plants in blocks 18 in. (45 cm.) apart.

The best variety is Lathom Self-Blanching.

Tomatoes

Bush varieties can be sown in blocks in March or early April, putting three seeds per block. Germinate the seeds in 60°F (15°C) and later reduce the temperature a little.

The plants can be set out under cloches in May, planting them in rows with one row per run of cloches. Set the plants 2 ft (60 cm.) apart and leave 3 ft (90 cm.) between the rows. The cloches can be removed during June or July to allow pollinating insects to do their job.

Fluid Sowing

Most of the work done at our research stations is naturally for the direct benefit of the commercial grower. Basically, they are there in order to develop a technology that will help reduce, or at least stabilise the cost of food.

Now and again, however, the techniques the scientists use in the early, small-scale trials, are ideally suited to the home gardener. Fluid sowing is just such a technique and though there are now special kits available, all you actually need can in fact be found in the kitchen and on the garage shelf. Where the commercial grower would use sophisticated and very expensive machinery, the home gardener can do exactly the same thing on a small scale, with a polythene bag and a sandwich box!

I suppose that the time which is fraught with the most anxiety for the gardener is the early spring when a large part of the valuable seed order is committed to the soil. Some seeds are easy. It is rare that radish, cabbages or turnips don't come up, regardless of the weather and soil conditions. Others cause an annual outbreak of nail-biting and furrowed brows.

If weather conditions are too wet or too cold, seeds are slow to germinate and may rot in the soil. And even in the summer there may be problems. Lettuce seed, for example, will not germinate when the soil temperature is too high. It is not at all uncommon for soil temperatures to rise above 77°F (25°C) in hot, dry summer weather. At this temperature an inhibitor in the seed coat prevents germination. If, however, the seeds can be germinated at a lower temperature and then sown, the seedlings will grow perfectly happily, even at higher temperatures.

The solution to both problems, is to germinate the seeds *first* in optimum conditions and then to sow them.

That is a simple matter with big seed. Anything like beans or peas, for example, can be pre-germinated in the greenhouse or in any warm spot in the house, picked up carefully and dropped into the seed drills outside. Even smaller seeds can be handled with tweezers, though this is, of course, a fiddly and time-consuming job. But, provided the tiny new root is undamaged the young seedlings will emerge in next to no time and grow away happily.

Handling small seeds is not so easy and it is for that reason that the technique of fluid sowing was developed.

Basically, the seeds are first pre-germinated in ideal conditions. They are then mixed with a jelly, stirred around to distribute them evenly, and then the jelly is squeezed out into the seed drills. This way, with the germinated seeds suspended in the jelly, the delicate young root (radicle) is undamaged and the seeds are evenly spread out down the

57. Put a piece of filter paper into a germinating dish

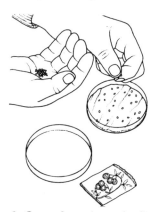

58. Space the seeds out evenly on the wet filter paper

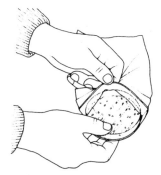

59. Replace the lid and put the dish in a polythene bag

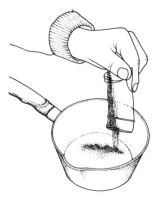

60. *Mix the special gel in a saucepan*

61. *Wash the germinated seeds gently into a sieve*

62. *Pour the mixture into a plastic container*

rows, reducing thinning out to a minimum.

Though all the materials needed for the job are readily available in most homes, life is made a little easier with a proprietary kit which can be bought quite cheaply at most good garden shops.

Germinating the seed

The three essentials for good germination are moisture, air and a little warmth. If these three factors are provided, there is a ninety per cent chance of good germination.

If you have a proprietary kit, the seeds can be evenly spread out on a piece of filter paper in the special plastic trays. If not, use a plastic sandwich box and a few sheets of absorbent paper. Before placing the seeds on the paper, cover it with water, allow it to soak it up and tip away the excess (57).

After spreading out the seeds (58), replace the lid of the container and place it in a polythene bag to ensure that the humidity inside is maintained (59). It should now be placed in a warm spot. I have found an airing cupboard to be ideal, but be warned – don't put the box immediately on top of the hot water cylinder. There it will be too hot and the seeds will simply dry out and fail to germinate. The first shelf will be plenty hot enough. About 70°F (21°C) is ideal.

Keep an eye on the seeds every day. The radicle will soon show – very often long before you expect it – and it is not a good thing to let it grow too long. If it does, it may well be damaged when it is stirred into the jelly. As a rough guide, most vegetable seeds should take between two to six days to germinate. The radicle of lettuces and smaller seeds should not be allowed to grow to much more than about $\frac{3}{16}$ths inch (4.5 mm.) long, while larger seeds can be allowed to grow no more than twice this length.

If the seeds germinate at an inconvenient time for sowing they can be stored in the refrigerator. Put them in the main part of the cabinet, *not* in the freezer cupboard, where they will be likely to suffer damage. Here they can stay for a day or two without making much growth and without being harmed.

When you are ready to sow them, the seeds must be removed very carefully from the box, ready to be mixed with the carrier fluid. The best way to do this is to gently wash them out under the tap, into a fine meshed sieve. Don't handle the seeds or they may be damaged (61).

Now the carrier fluid should be prepared. If you buy a proprietary kit, it will contain a small sachet of alginate gel. This must be mixed with water and heated whilst stirring continually (60). It will eventually form a thin jelly, when it can be removed and allowed to cool. The do-it-yourselfer can make his own gel with ordinary wallpaper paste. Choose one without an added fungicide, and mix it to about half-strength. Wallpaper paste, of course, does not need heating. Just mix it as you would for wallpapering, but to half the recommended strength.

Tip half the gel into a basin, add the seeds, and then the other half of the gel.

Mix them round very gently to get them evenly distributed. Some gardeners prefer to do this with their fingers to avoid damage, but I have found that the careful use of a wooden spoon does no harm. When the seeds are in the gel, they should remain suspended. If they sink to the bottom, the mixture is too thin.

Now transfer the mixture to the container used to distribute the seeds (62). A proprietary kit will contain a plastic bottle with a couple of nozzles of different sizes. A wide-nozzled cake syringe will do just as well, or you can use a polythene bag. Simply pour in the liquid, tie the top and cut off one corner.

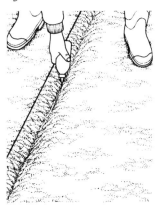

63. *Draw a drill with a hoe*

Sowing

Outside, prepare a seed drill in the normal way (63). In dry weather, it is wise to pour a little water down the drill before sowing. Seeds should never be sown into dry soil, and this is particularly important when fluid sowing.

Walk backwards down the row, gently squeezing the container to spread the fluid evenly (64). A 30 ft (9 m.) row should take about $\frac{1}{4}$ pt (140 ml.) of gel, and this should contain about the right number of seeds for a thin sowing.

Cover the seeds with soil in the normal way and tamp it down lightly with the back of a rake. Unless the soil is quite moist, it is important to water after sowing. I did deliberately neglect to do so on one sowing at Barnsdale during hot, dry weather. The seed failed to germinate and when it was uncovered the gel had become quite hard, with the seed trapped inside. The seeds should emerge in just a few days, and from then on they can be treated normally.

64. *Squeeze the seeds out of the bottle down the row*

Sowing tomatoes outside

One of the more interesting applications of fluid sowing is in the raising of bush tomatoes by direct sowing outside.

Normally tomatoes are grown from plants raised in a heated greenhouse from an April sowing or bought in from the nurseryman. These are transplanted outside in June, and will crop sometime during July or August, depending on location.

This is quite an expensive method and it does require heated glass which all gardeners do not have. An alternative method is to sow the seeds direct outside under cloches (65). If they are fluid sown they will emerge very quickly, and will crop only a little later than those from plants raised in heat.

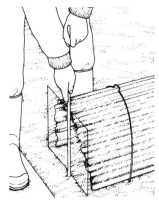

65. *Tomatoes can be sown outside under cloches*

Varieties

It is essential to choose the right variety. It must be a bush type (one that does not need to have the side-shoots removed) and it must be an early ripening variety. I found the best results with the relatively new variety Sub Arctic Plenty. The plants are compact, and the fruits, though small, are very sweet. From a mid-to-late-May sowing, they will crop in about 55 days and somewhat earlier if they are grown under cloches or a polythene tunnel.

For slightly later crops, the National Vegetable Research Station recommend Sleaford Abundance or Sigmabush which will ripen within 65–70 days of planting. Even later is the variety Alfresco which takes from 70–90 days to ripen. The fruits of this variety are somewhat larger than the others.

I found little advantage in growing the later crops. In a bad tomato year when the weather is cold and dull there is a risk that the plants may not ripen before the first frosts – this is more of a danger in the north of the country. The earlier maturing variety cropped at Barnsdale until early November and provided more than enough fruits.

It is possible to sow the seeds outside from about the last week in April – a little later in the north – without the use of cloches. There is some risk with this method that the young plants may be damaged by late spring frosts. The experience of the NVRS is that the risk is low and is certainly worth taking in the more favoured areas of the country.

Being in the Midlands, and in a fairly exposed spot, I decided not to risk the dangers of frost damage, and sowed a little earlier under cloches.

The cloches were placed over the soil in early April, a couple of weeks before sowing, in order to warm the ground up first. I prepared the ground well first, digging in plenty of manure, and applying Growmore at 4 oz per sq. yd (120 gm per sq. m.). I also raised the soil a little so as to ensure that it did not lie wet. This has the effect of warming it up and warm roots are, in my opinion, one of the secrets of successful tomato growing.

A few days before you are ready to sow start the seeds off in the airing cupboard in the manner described, and when they are germinated, transfer them to a carrier jelly.

Before sowing the soil should be prepared and a liquid fertiliser should be applied.

The NVRS recommend 1¼ oz (35 gm) of 'Kaynitro' plus 2 oz (57 gm) of triple superphosphate mixed in 2½ gallons (11.35 litres) of water. In practice I found this difficult to obtain, so I stuck my neck out and varied it slightly. I used the same proportions, but for the Kaynitro I substituted a proprietary tomato base fertiliser, and for the triple superphosphate, I used plain superphosphate. It seemed to work perfectly well. In fact, the need with the starter fertiliser is for a high content of phosphates to stimulate root growth and, provided this requirement is met, there seems to be some room for manoeuvre.

The fertiliser should be thoroughly mixed the night before use and allowed to stand. Not all of it will dissolve, but what is left can remain in the bottom of the can.

The fertiliser should be applied directly beneath the seeds, but it is not a good thing to allow them to come into contact with it immediately. The drill should therefore be made a little deeper than is necessary, so that the fertiliser can be poured in and covered over with a little more soil before sowing.

The seeds can now be sown, squeezing out two or three seeds in a clump, spacing the clumps about 1 ft (30 cm.) apart down the row. Under normal-sized cloches, it will only be possible to get in one row of plants.

The seedlings will take about a week to a fortnight to emerge. There will be at least two and probably three seedlings in each clump but there is no need to thin them out. In fact, three plants grown close together will make the same sized bush as one plant on its own and yields will not be reduced.

During the growing season there is very little to do. It is not necessary to feed bush tomatoes in the way that you would those grown as vines up canes. Too much nitrogen will induce excessive growth and this could have the effect of reducing yields. Make sure that the crop never goes short of water. This will almost certainly mean removing the cloches to apply water by hand. In fact, I found that by early July the cloches were unnecessary, and it was much easier to water and weed without them, so they were removed. They were replaced in late September when the weather became wet and cold, and early frosts threatened.

Though the plants should not be allowed to dry out, watering should be avoided if possible in the early stages. If too much water is applied, this also has the effect of increasing foliage and stem growth at the expense of fruit. Once the plants start to flower regular watering at about 1 gal. per sq. yd (4.5 litres per sq. m.) will have a considerable effect on the yield.

In the early stages it will be necessary to control weeds by hand. Later on, the plants will become very bushy and will completely cover the ground and smother the weeds.

It is advisable, once the plants start to fruit, to apply a mulch of straw or peat around them. When the stems become weighted down with fruit, they will touch the soil. A mulch will help to keep the fruit clean, and will discourage the attentions of slugs.

The only important pests that are likely to be encountered

are aphids, and these can easily be controlled with a proprietary greenfly killer. Birds may also be a problem, and the only way to prevent them getting to the fruit before you do, is to cover them with netting.

The plants should start cropping from mid-July or thereabouts, and will continue until they are cut down by the first frosts. They should produce something like 2–4 lbs of fruit per plant.

Transplants

If you have the use of a cold-frame, it is possible to raise even earlier plants and to transplant them to the open ground later.

Sow the seeds in the cold frame in the way described previously but from the beginning of April. Instead of squeezing out the fluid in 'stations', it is best to sow these in straightforward rows, leaving about 4 in. (10 cm.) between rows.

The plants can be transplanted when they are about 6–8 in. (15–20 cm.) high. I was quite surprised at the ease with which they transplant. They are certainly as successful as young cabbage plants and I found one hundred per cent of them grew away successfully after transplanting. At Barnsdale we managed to plant out by the end of May and the plants were every bit as good as those raised expensively in the heated greenhouse.

New Crops

Cut-and-Come-Again Lettuce

An experiment we tried with great success, produced vast quantities of 'leaf-lettuce' in a relatively small space. We did, in fact, also achieve a succession of leaves from the last week in May through to the last week in October. All this, in a space of 5 sq. yds (4.2 sq. m.).

There are several varieties of leaf-lettuce available from the seed catalogues. Salad Bowl is probably the most popular. We used two conventional hearted types but grew them in a different way.

The method was devised by the National Vegetable Research Station, and dubbed, 'Cut-and-come-again' lettuce. The greatest advantage of this method is the fact that an area similar to the one I sowed at Barnsdale, will produce the equivalent of five hearted lettuce every week. For conventional crops of hearted lettuce, you would need at least twice that area.

The crop is harvested much earlier than usual too, so the first lettuce in May can be grown without the aid of cloches. Added to this I found the crop quite labour-saving. If the seed is sown thinly, there is no need to thin out the seedlings. The close growth also tends to crowd out the weeds.

There is another hidden advantage that didn't occur to me until I went on holiday. Before going, I cut a number of crisp leaves to take with me to last a couple of days. When I returned, the stumps of the cut plants had produced another crop of leaves all ready to eat. Not a bad service, I thought.

Varieties

It is important to choose your varieties carefully. The NVRS have found that some varieties produce rather bitter leaves when they are grown in this way. I tried Lobjoits Green Cos and Avoncrisp and didn't notice a sign of bitterness. I must say, that I also preferred the crispness of the leaves compared with the conventional leaf-lettuce varieties. For the later sowings, it is suggested that the variety Avondefiance be substituted for Avoncrisp. It has much more resistance to lettuce mildew, which is prevalent later in the year, especially when the plants are grown at this close spacing. I grew Avoncrisp and Lobjoits right the way through the season, with no sign of trouble, but I wouldn't like to suggest that this is the wisest thing to do everywhere.

The Method

There is nothing simpler than growing lettuce by this method. Prepare the land in the same way you would for hearted varieties. Rake it down to a fine, level tilth and rake in a dressing of Growmore at 2 oz per sq. yd (60 gm per sq. m.). The NVRS recommend using Nitrochalk, but I used Growmore in order to standardise as far as possible all my work on the veg. plot. Too much nitrogen can produce bitterness in the leaves, so don't overdo the application, whichever chemical you use.

Sow the seeds in shallow drills spaced 5 in. (12 cm.) apart. Make the sowing fairly light. All you need is 12–15 plants per 1 ft (30 cm.) run. Since at most times of the year, you would expect about 80 per cent germination, a thin sowing is all that is needed. If the soil contains little moisture, run a little water into the seed drill before sowing.

Keep the rows free from weeds in the early stages and later on the leafy growth will suppress most weeds. Other than that it should only be necessary to provide sufficient water when the soil is dry.

Harvesting takes place from 40–50 days after sowing, depending on the time of the year. Naturally, in the cooler spring and autumn weather, they take a little longer than those plants sown in the summer.

When you need some leaves, simply cut them off with a sharp knife, leaving about 1 in. (2.5 cm.) of stem (66). Then clean any old leaves or weeds from around the base of the plants and water the soil well. After a week or two, the stems will start to produce another set of leaves and these can be grown on and harvested in the same way.

It is not wise to allow more than one lot of regrowth to occur. The old stumps would continue to push out new leaves, but they might also contain more than their fair share of pests and diseases. So it is best to sow again, timing the sowing so that you are never without fresh leaves.

To maintain a continuity of supply, you will need to make only half the number of sowings you would for conventional, hearted lettuce.

If you start sowing at the beginning of April and do so at weekly intervals until the middle of May, you can then rely on the regrowth to provide the next set of leaves. Then start sowing again in the first week in August, making two more sowings, again with a week's interval. All being well, and obviously depending upon the length of the rows, you should have fresh lettuce leaves for your salads from May to the end of October or even into November.

Leafless peas

One of the functions of Barnsdale, is to try out as many new vegetable, flower and fruit varieties as I have space for. All too often, the 'improvements' are really not a lot better than the old, tried varieties. Sometimes they are not as good. But once in a while, our trials throw up a real winner.

66. *Cut the lettuces, leaving an inch of stem*

Leafless peas seem, at first sight, to have no advantage for the amateur gardener. They were originally bred for the farmers who grow for the canning industry because they are much easier to harvest mechanically. Harvesting causes no problems for the home gardener. Indeed, pea picking is one of those pleasant jobs not to be delegated on a bright summer morning.

I tried the new leafless variety Bikini and was pleasantly surprised. Perhaps the greatest advantage was that the plants were self-supporting and needed no staking. They grow to only about 2 ft (60 cm.) high, and the mass of tendrils they produce in place of leaves, holds them all up in a mass. I sowed three rows together, so that they formed a completely self-supporting block.

Picking is simple even though the plants produce a veritable forest of tendril growth. The crop is borne right at the top of the plant, actually above the growth, so it is easy to see the full pods and to get at them.

The crop was good, certainly as good as other varieties and the peas were sweet and of excellent texture. A new variety I can confidently recommend.

Abyssinian cabbage

A recent expedition to Ethiopia brought back this entirely new vegetable to British gardeners. You may well think that a plant from such a hot part of the world would not do well in our climate, but at Barnsdale it really flourished. So much so, in fact, that I found it somewhat difficult to keep up with. The leaves are supposed to be harvested when they are no more than about 6 in. (15 cm.) high.

Mine grew so well that, by the time the cameras arrived for me to show this new discovery to the world, they had reached about 4 ft (120 cm.). One of my more notable disasters!

I suppose the nearest way to describe Abyssinian cabbage is to liken it to our own spring cabbage. But this one will crop right through the summer, giving a mass of tender, flavoursome leaves, with a slightly more tangy taste than cabbage.

The seeds are sown from early spring onwards in rows no more than 6 in. (15 cm.) apart. It is necessary to give them this sort of competition to prevent them from romping away and growing coarse. The leaves are picked when they are very young and can easily be grown in succession to provide young leaves throughout the summer.

Rhubarb

I made two good rhubarb discoveries in the course of the *Gardeners' World* trials. The first was a new variety called Cawood Delight. Bred at the Stockbridge House Experimental Horticultural Station, it is bound to be a winner at shows and in the kitchen. Not only are the long stems red right up to the base of the leaves, but when they are cut, the red colouring goes right through the inside too and is retained after cooking. Flavour is excellent and the plants proved as prolific as other varieties. Watch out for it.

But perhaps my biggest surprise came from planting virus-tested rhubarb plants. I can only assume that the majority of rhubarb grown in British gardens is infected with virus diseases, because the virus-free stock grew with a vigour and to a size that was nothing short of staggering. Virus-tested stock is now available to home gardeners, and I can guarantee that you will be amazed at the difference.

But of course, like all virus-free plants, the problem is to *keep* them free from disease. Stockbridge House EHS have published some guidelines which are well worth noting. Since virus diseases are spread to some extent by tiny soil organisms, clean stock should not be planted in soil that has grown rhubarb before. Remember that viruses can live for long periods in the soil, so even waiting for several years will not do.

Try also to avoid growing new plants near to members of the cabbage family. They are notorious for attracting aphids – the second carrier of the diseases. And of course, at the first sign of an aphid attack, spray the plants with a greenfly killer.

To get the best out of the new virus-tested plants, it is worth taking a little trouble over soil preparation and subsequent cultivation.

Make sure, first of all, that the soil is well drained. Rhubarb will do tolerably well even on poor soil, but it cannot abide wet feet.

There is a popular misconception that rhubarb prefers an acid soil. I suppose this may have come about because of the acidic nature of the plant. Nothing, however, could be further from the truth. Before planting, it is well worth testing your soil for its lime content. A pH of 7.0 is ideal so it may be quite likely that liming will be necessary. Bear in mind also that it may take several years to correct acidity, so you may need to lime annually for several years. Before planting, rake in a dressing of Growmore at 4 oz per sq. yd (120 gm per sq. m.).

The biggest yield per square yard will be achieved by spacing the plants in rows 3 ft (1 m.) apart, with 2½ ft (75 cm.) between plants. If the drainage is suspect, plant on ridges.

Plants grown in containers are available at many garden centres and these can be planted at any time of the year. In the winter and early spring, they will have no leaves, so care before planting and immediately afterwards is simple. Simply water the plants well before removing them from the pots, plant them with a trowel and firm them in with your heel. They should be planted so that there is about 1 in. (2.5 cm.) of soil covering the crowns.

If you buy plants in the summer, attention must be paid to watering if you can't get them planted straight away (67). If the plants remain in the containers for long, they will also need to be fed with a liquid fertiliser at weekly intervals.

It is a good idea with large, leafy plants, to cut off the very large leaves before planting, to reduce water loss. Make sure also, that if the weather is dry, the plants are well watered in, and that they do not go dry before they have had a chance to get well rooted.

During the season, make sure that weeds are kept down, by regular hoeing.

Do not remove any sticks for the first year. After that, you can pull as you wish, though it is never wise to strip the plants completely. Top-dress each March with Growmore at 3 oz per sq. yd (90 gm per sq. m.), and the plants will go on producing happily for anything up to ten years.

67. Pot-grown rhubarb must be watered well before planting

Weed Control

In recent years, weedkillers have had a bad press. The very word 'herbicide' has become associated with the defoliation of trees in Vietnam, large-scale disasters in Italy and the accidental destruction of crops by spray drift the world over. That's a pity, because it really has very little to do with garden weedkillers.

Certainly, the vast majority of agricultural herbicides are dangerous if used wrongly. Of course, if you drink half a gallon of paraquat it will kill you. But then so would half a gallon of Scotch!

But weedkillers sold to gardeners are a very different formulation to those used by professional growers and farmers, and all are very much less potent. It is true to say that, if they are used according to the manufacturer's instructions, they are harmless. And they can be a real boon to both the professional grower and the amateur gardener. Bear in mind too, that *all* the fruit and vegetables you buy from the greengrocer have been grown with the help of herbicides, and there is no evidence that they cause any harm to the consumers.

Of course, we gardeners do not have the range of herbicides that the professional has, but there are enough about now to cover most garden weeding. It will still be necessary to use the hoe to a large extent but you could certainly reduce the work by half with the use of weedkillers.

Perennial weeds
Anyone who has taken over an allotment riddled with couch grass or bellbine will know the problems caused by perennial weeds. Frankly, you can dig the plot over two spades deep, removing every bit of the roots below and it will still come back as strongly as ever. During the first few seasons, it is virtually impossible to keep on top of the task of hoeing and consequently crops are greatly reduced. This has often been the cause of a keen gardener simply giving up.

The golden rule is to start clean, even if it takes the first year to get it that way. There are one or two weedkillers available that will clean unplanted land completely, so that you never need be troubled again.

If couch grass is the problem, and there are no other perennial weeds, Dalapon is the answer.

This is a specific grass killer and does an excellent job of killing couch. It should be sprayed or watered on when the grass is growing vigorously. After a couple of weeks, the land should be cultivated as deeply as possible and the couch allowed to regrow. A second spray should see it off.

If other weeds are present, it is better to use a weedkiller containing glyphosate. Murphy produce one called 'Tumbleweed'. This will kill all perennial and annual weeds. It is a translocated herbicide, which is scientific jargon for saying that it is absorbed through the leaves and passes down to the roots. It has the action of preventing the roots from storing food, so eventually the plant starves. This means that it takes a little time to work effectively, so after spraying, the weeds should be left alone for at least ten days.

Spray when the plants are in active growth and try to put on as little as possible. Once the spray starts to run off the leaves it has less effect. Aim to apply it in small droplets that will hang on to the foliage while it is absorbed. The makers suggest that it can be applied with a watering can, but this is certainly not the most effective way. And, since the chemical is not cheap, it is also a costly way of doing it.

Annual Weeds

Once perennial weeds are killed, it should not be difficult to keep them at bay. But you will still be troubled by annuals. The problem is made worse by bad husbandry. All annual weeds should be killed or removed before they have a chance to seed. Remember that one plant is capable of spreading hundreds or even thousands of seeds, each of which is likely to produce a new plant. In the absence of competition from perennials they rule the roost, and will quickly take over. I make a habit of hoeing through my vegetable plot once a week, *whether there are weeds there or not*. This ensures that they are killed, often even before they have emerged, and certainly before they begin to compete with the cultivated crops.

But I would never have time to do this without killing what weeds I can, with chemical weedkillers.

All annual weeds around the edges of the plot, and anywhere else where no cultivated crops are growing can be killed with a mixture of paraquat and diquat. This is sold by ICI as Weedol.

It acts on the mechanism that makes chlorophyll – the green colouring in leaves and stems. Without this, the plant cannot manufacture food and so dies. During the summer it is very effective and quick. It can also be used in the winter, but takes some time to show any effect. Bear in mind that it is in no way selective. It will kill crops as effectively as it kills weeds if you allow any to fall on the leaves. So, it must be used with care.

I have used it very effectively on vegetables that take a long time to germinate. This can be a bit of a risky business, but if you allow plenty of margin for error, it works like a dream.

The land at Barnsdale was infested with chickweed in the first two years. As you know, this pernicious annual seeds

68. *Weed killers are best applied with a sprayer*

itself very readily, even in the winter and it is extremely difficult to keep up with by hoeing. The greatest problem was with seeds like parsnip that take anything up to six weeks to emerge. The chickweed was established down the rows long before that, and it was difficult to find the parsnip seedlings when they finally did show themselves.

My solution was to make a careful note of the sowing date and then to spray the weed seedlings in the parsnip rows five weeks after sowing. When the parsnips came through, the land was as clean as a whistle, and I had the best crop ever.

In the second year I got cold feet and decided that I was taking too much of a risk. I sprayed that year, four weeks after sowing, and the effect was the same. The weed seeds that were in the ground had obviously not had a chance to germinate before the parsnips showed through. I now use that technique every year.

There are two pre-emergence weedkillers available to gardeners that, though they cannot be used on all crops, will certainly cut your weeding time in half.

Simazine can be sprayed on the soil after planting many crops. It has the effect of killing annual weed seedlings as they emerge, so it will keep your soil completely clean, often through the life of the crop. I did notice just one disadvantage with this one. It acts by forming a crust on the soil surface. If that crust is broken by walking on the soil, weeds tend to grow in the footprints. It is therefore important to keep off the soil once it is sprayed.

Simazine is also used in several path weedkillers. Here it is formulated for total weed control, and generally mixed with other chemicals. It should not be used in the vegetable garden at all. Murphy make one for pre-emergence control in the vegetable garden, and this is called 'Weedex'.

Propachlor is another pre-emergence weedkiller for use on a variety of crops. I have used it on onions, leeks and all members of the cabbage family with great success. The manufacturers also claim that it can be used on runner and dwarf beans, though I have never tried this.

Murphy market propachlor under the trade name 'Covershield'.

All these weedkillers can be used in the vegetable garden with complete confidence. But they *must* be stored, mixed and applied strictly according to the manufacturer's instructions.

Pests and Diseases

Of the hundreds of pests and diseases likely to invade the productive garden, most are easy to control. There are plenty of insecticides and fungicides available to the home gardener and information on their uses is easy to come by. But there are two catagories that are not so easy. The first is the virus diseases that have so far beaten even the best of our boffins, who have been researching into their whys and wherefores for many years.

The only counter-measure against viruses, seems to be to prevent an attack before it starts. The first golden rule is to start with clean stock. Never accept from a friend a plant that is subject to virus attack. Many fruit trees and bushes and such things as potatoes, are covered by a Ministry of Agriculture certification scheme that guarantees that the plants are free from virus disease when they leave the raiser's premises. The wise gardener buys nothing but a certified plant wherever the scheme applies.

But as soon as the plant is in your garden, there is no guarantee that it will not immediately become infected with a virus disease. So regular preventative action must be taken.

The arch criminal in the gardening underworld, is the greenfly. As you know, rarely a summer goes by without a visit from at least a few thousand of these little monsters and every one could be a carrier of a virus. They only have to stop for lunch and your plants could become infected.

So, it is essential to keep an eagle eye open for the first sign of attack, and to take prompt action to eradicate the pests. There are plenty of aphicides (the up-market term for greenfly killers) available, which will only kill aphids. These are infinitely preferable to the more general insecticides, since they will not harm other insects, many of which are natural predators of greenfly and other undesirables.

You should learn to recognise the symptoms of virus diseases. Some plants have specific symptoms but all will show a decrease in size and vigour, and generally a yellowing of the foliage. If other plants are doing well, and the soil is fertile, suspect virus disease.

When it appears you must harden your heart. It is always difficult to pull a plant up and throw it away, especially if it has served you well, but that is precisely what must be done. And the sooner it is done, the better. Don't put it on the compost heap where it can contaminate the compost and eventually the soil. The only place for virus diseases is the bonfire.

At Barnsdale we have not had a lot of trouble with virus diseases – or at least so I thought – then I got hold of some virus-tested rhubarb. The difference in growth and vigour is quite extraordinary, so I must assume that the majority of rhubarb sold is already infected with the disease. Virus-tested stock is now available to the amateur gardener, and it's well worth searching it out.

One of the general pieces of advice given when virus diseases are detected is, 're-plant in another part of the garden'. Well, I am far from convinced that this does any good at all. Virus diseases are microscopic and exist in their billions. All that would be necessary to spread the disease would be to take a piece of soil the size of a pin-head from infected to non-infected land, and the disease would spread like wildfire.

On the other hand, since viruses can live in the soil almost indefinitely, there seems little else one can do.

The second catagory of pests and diseases that are not that easy to control, are those that live and do their dirty work in the soil. From the *Gardeners' World* postbag we know that they cause more problems for gardeners than the rest of them put together. So I have done a couple of trials on cabbage root fly and carrot fly, based mainly on the work done by the NVRS. I have also had a look at clubroot control, though not at Barnsdale. I am not troubled with it there, and I am certainly not going to import it for the sake of a trial.

Cabbage Root Fly

For the cabbage root fly experiment I grew eight rows of cabbage and repeated the same trial with eight rows of cauliflower. As you probably know, cauliflower are the most prone to attack, and the worst affected.

The first three rows were treated with proprietary soil insecticides. I used diazinon (Fisons Soil Insecticide), chlorpyriphos (Murphy Soil Pest Killer), and bromophos (PBI Bromophos). The fourth and fifth rows were devoted to old gardener's remedies.

In one I put a piece of rhubarb in the planting hole and in the other a couple of moth-balls.

The plants in the next row were protected physically, by placing a bit of foam rubber round the stem (69). The last two rows were untreated, as a control.

The results were interesting. The first trial failed completely because for the first time for years, the cabbage root fly decided to give Barnsdale a miss. That's the Law of the Cussedness of Nature we gardeners all know so well. But for the second trial, they were good enough to grace me with their presence.

The two untreated rows went down like ninepins showing the typical wilting. When the plants were pulled up, they were crawling with the root-fly maggots.

The two rows treated with moth balls and rhubarb also,

I'm afraid, succumbed to attack. Devastation of those two rows was complete, with not a plant left untouched. So, another couple of gardening myths down the drain, I'm afraid.

All three chemically-treated rows escaped with the exception of one plant treated with bromophos.

I treated all the plants in the same way with each of the chemicals. Before planting, I raked them into the soil surface. However, none of the three are credited with such persistance that they will last in the soil through the life of the plant. So, about a fortnight after planting, I also sprinkled a little chemical round the base of the stems. Of the three, I personally prefer diazinon or chlorpyriphos, since they are formulated as granules and are therefore likely to last longer. However, all three gave very good control.

The physical barrier of foam rubber also gave complete control and is therefore an excellent method, particularly if you would prefer to use chemicals only as a last resort. Again developed in the course of much wider research by the NVRS, this is an ideal method for the amateur, though ironically, quite useless for the commercial grower. Those blokes simply don't have the time to mess about with bits of foam rubber on fifty acres of cauliflower!

The idea of the foam rubber is to prevent the adult fly laying her eggs close to the stem of the plant. Normally, she would squat on the soil and place her egg tube down near the plant. When the eggs hatch out they then have an immediate source of food. If there is a physical barrier to prevent this, she'll fly away and have a go at your next-door neighbour's cabbages.

The foam rubber is simply foam-based carpet underfelt. Again, I polished up my brass neck and asked at the carpet shop for a few off-cuts. They were only too pleased to give me enough to treat that fifty acres. The underfelt is cut into squares about 6 in. (15 cm.) across, and a slit is cut from the centre to one side. I then made a *very small* cross cut so that the stem would fit without buckling the foam. It is important to make this a small cut. After the trial, I had a few queries from viewers for whom the method hadn't worked. On investigation, I found that in every case, the hole in the centre had been too big.

Another advantage with this method is that it also provides a home for small ground beetles, whose diet consists of cabbage root fly larvae, so it really is a 'belt and braces' job.

69. *Foam-rubber squares prevent the cabbage root-fly laying its eggs*

Carrot Fly

I used the same set-up and the same three chemicals for the carrot fly trial. If there is one thing that is guaranteed at Barnsdale, it's a visit from carrot fly. The grubs burrow into the roots of carrots and parsnips, making unsightly tunnels, causing adult plants to wilt and killing off seedlings completely.

Apart from the chemical control, I also tried the accepted gardener's dodge of sowing alternate rows of carrots and onions. The idea here is that, since the adult flies are attracted by smell, they would become confused by the smell of the onions. Alas, it doesn't work. In my trials, all the untreated rows were attacked, including those sown between the onions.

The chemical controls proved successful. Again, I made two applications with about a fortnight between them, and only a very few of the plants were affected. Again, these were those treated with bromophos.

Two other factors can help in controlling the flies. Firstly, try to plant as far away from hedging as possible. When the flies are not abroad doing their worst, that's where they live.

Your plants will be most vulnerable to attack at thinning time. When the seedlings are handled, the smell is at its strongest, and will set any local fly's mouth watering. The best time to thin is in the evening or on a dull, overcast day. And never, never leave the thinnings lying about. Pick them all up and put them on the compost heap with a covering of soil.

At the end of the growing season, lift both carrots and parsnips and store them, since flies can attack quite late in the year.

Clubroot

The very word 'clubroot' strikes dread into the heart of the dedicated vegetable gardener. It must be one of the most debilitating and difficult to control of all diseases. Once clubroot spores penetrate the roots of members of the cabbage family and a few related species, they cause swellings on the roots and severly affect the plant's growth.

Like viruses, the best bet is avoidance. Again, never accept plants from friends, unless you are certain they do not come from infected land. Never even borrow a spade or a pair of boots that have been anywhere near an infected garden. Even they could spread the disease.

Without wishing to suggest that there is no hope at all of controlling the disease, it must be accepted that complete control is so far impossible, and partial control difficult.

There is a widespread belief that if you avoid growing susceptible plants for seven years, the life cycle will be broken and the disease will die out. Alas, another myth. Spores of clubroot can exist in the soil, even if there is no host plant present, for as long as twenty years. Rotation is not to be entirely scorned in a large garden, but in most there simply is not enough room to be able to isolate plants from the spread of the disease.

So, if you are unlucky enough to be plagued by clubroot, you must simply learn to live with it. There are steps that can be taken to reduce the effects of the disease.

Firstly, ensure that your land is adequately limed. Get hold of a soil test kit – the lime testing kits are quite cheap and very accurate – and add lime to the soil each year to bring the pH to about 7. Improving the soil drainage will also help.

There are one or two chemicals that have proved useful and these should be used in the form of a root dip at planting time. Benomyl (PBI Benlate), calomel dust and thiophanate methyl (Murphy Club Root Dip) have all proved effective in reducing the effects of the disease (70).

70. *Dipping brassica seedlings before planting helps control clubroot*

Another way to reduce the effects, though it does nothing towards effecting a cure, is to raise the plants in pots. Use either sterilised soil, or a proprietary potting compost, and grow the plants on to an advanced stage in 6 in. (15 cm.) pots. The root ball will be unaffected and, even though subsequent roots made after planting out may be attacked, the plant will be able to survive and produce a reasonable crop.

To prevent the spread of the disease, plants should be lifted as soon as they are harvested, and the stumps burned.

Japanese Onions

There are few crops more important on the gardener's list than onions. In the kitchen, they are one of the most versatile and necessary vegetables, being used for everything from soups to pies.

Add to that the fact that onions will store almost until the new crop is ready to harvest, and they become an essential in the self-respecting vegetable plot. But it's that 'almost' that is annoying and frustrating. In every gardener's calendar there comes a time when he must go out and buy foreign onions from the greengrocer or use his shallots, because those in store have gone soft and the new crop is not quite ready to harvest.

With this gap in mind, much research has gone on into means of bridging the crucial weeks between June and August. The plant breeders and the seedsmen have been at work to provide a variety that will crop as early as the end of June. They have come up with a selection of Japanese varieties that, on the whole, fill the bill very well.

These new varieties are sown in August, and overwintered for maturing the following June or July. Of course this is not a new principle at all. For centuries gardeners have been sowing at that time and overwintering with varying degrees of success. But there are problems with the old varieties. First of all, the losses during a hard winter are likely to be great, and this is more noticeable on soils with a high organic matter content. This system also tends to produce a high proportion of 'bolters', or plants that run to seed, and that ruins the bulb for use in the kitchen. But the greatest disadvantage of all is that, even when overwintered, the older varieties still mature in August, or in late July at best. For early onions, it has to be the new varieties.

Varieties
There are several new varieties now appearing in the seedsmen's catalogues, and more seem to be added each year. It is well worth trying a row or two of something new each year, but the following varieties are tried and tested.

Express Yellow is an Fı hybrid variety that will mature from early to mid-June. Like all Japanese varieties, it is lighter in colour and flatter than most European types.

Imai Yellow will mature in late June or early July. It is paler in colour than Express Yellow and slightly more globe-shaped. Senshyu Semi-Globe Yellow matures from mid-to-late July. It is flatter than the other varieties but has a deeper skin colour.

All these varieties have the same pungent smell and flavour of the European types but they do not keep as well.

They should, therefore, only be grown for summer use. Aim to grow enough to last the couple of months before the main crop of European varieties is ready to harvest.

Sowing

The time of sowing is critical. Remember that it is no use sowing these varieties in the spring since they will not produce bulbs large enough for use. To do that, they need to get away to a good start in the late summer, and to be all ready to grow away again as soon as weather conditions permit in the early spring.

The plants must also be large enough to withstand a possible hard winter, so the correct sowing date is important. The aim should be to get the plants to 6–8 in. (15–20 cm.) high before the end of October when they virtually stop growing. However, if they are sown too early, they will simply run to seed before they are harvested.

Weather conditions vary considerably throughout the country, so seed must be sown earlier in the north than in the south and south-west. As a general guide, sow by early August in Scotland and the far north of England. In the Midlands and the east, sowing should be completed by the middle of the month, while the end of August is early enough if you live in the south.

Before sowing, rake the soil to a fine, firm tilth, and rake in Growmore at 4 oz per sq. yd (120 gm per sq. m.). In August, the soil is likely to be dry. If it is, run a can of water down the seed drill *before* sowing. Don't sow and then water or the top of the soil will form a crust which is harmful to the young seedlings.

Try not to water again until the seedlings emerge, unless the soil is drying out very fast, when it is better to do so.

Sow the seed thinly in shallow rows and firm by tamping down with the back of the rake afterwards. The seedlings should appear within seven to ten days. From then on, keep them completely weed-free, and make sure that they are not allowed to dry out. Remember, the aim is to get them to a good size before the winter sets in.

One of the essentials with Japanese onions and one of the reasons for the failure of many gardeners, is feeding. One of the 'old-wives-tales' that continues to persist, is that plants should never be fed nitrogen just before the winter and certainly not during it. Well, this may be so for some, more tender plants, but it is a theory that is being disproved for many subjects. With Japanese onions, nitrogen during the winter is *essential*, and it will *not* make the foliage too soft to stand the winter cold. Without it, the plants may stop growing completely during the winter, and there is a strong likelihood that they will run to seed as soon as the spring surge of growth begins.

So, a feed with a nitrogen fertiliser must be given during January. Use nitro-chalk, at 2–3 oz per sq. yd (60–90 gm per sq. m.) and lightly hoe it into the soil between the rows. Don't hoe too deeply or too close to the onions or the root systems may be damaged.

In February or March, the plants should be thinned to 2 in. (5 cm.) apart. Don't be tempted to do this before the early spring, since there could still be some losses due to wet, cold weather at the beginning of the year.

If your soil is light and peaty, losses may be more severe. Make sure that the soil around the plants is firm, even if it means treading it down again after severe frosts.

Another cause of winter loss – perhaps the greatest of all – is bad drainage. If the plants have cold, wet feet they will suffer in the winter just as you and I would. If your soil is badly-drained and likely to stand wet in the winter, grow your Japanese onions on the deep-bed, where the drainage will be considerably better.

After thinning in the spring, there is very little to do other than to keep the plants weed-free.

All onions hate competition from weeds, so that really is important. One of the new herbicides can be used effectively to control weeds in onions, and this is described on p. 52.

Spring-sown plants

Gardeners with a small vegetable plot generally dislike overwintered crops. They get in the way of the winter digging, and they have to be fitted into an already complicated successional sowing plan. On top of that, there is always the faint risk of the losses during a hard winter being too large, and of the plants running to seed in the spring.

An alternative method of raising Japanese onions is to sow in the heated greenhouse in early January and to plant out, after hardening off, in late March or April. There are obvious disadvantages. Firstly, valuable and expensive heat is necessary, though, if you intend to use the greenhouse during the winter for other crops, this may be a good way of making the most use of the heat. The system is more time-consuming than late summer sowing, but the biggest snag of all is that the onions will mature later than the summer-sown crop.

Sow the seed as early in January as possible, in a temperature of 60°F (15°C). About four weeks after germination, the temperature can be reduced to 55°F (13°C).

Transplant the seedlings when they are large enough to handle into seed trays, putting about 40 in each box. The aim should be to keep the plants growing as fast as possible during this time, without letting them become drawn and spindly. As with all plants in the greenhouse in the winter, it is not a bit of good increasing the heat if the light is poor.

This will not produce sturdy, healthy growth. So, make sure that the greenhouse glass is spotlessly clean, and put the onion plants as near to the glass as possible.

In mid-March, transfer the plants to the cold-frame for hardening off. This should be done gradually, increasing the ventilation a little more each day and night, until the lights can be removed altogether.

By April, they should be 6–8 in. (15–20 cm.) high, and have a strong, healthy root system. They are then ready for planting out.

Ideally, the plants should be planted in a bed, 6 in. (15 cm.) apart. If you prefer rows for weeding purposes, plant 4 in. (10 cm.) apart with 12 in. (30 cm.) between the rows. The same cultural methods should be used now as for the summer-sown crop.

We tried the two systems side-by-side at Barnsdale, and both crops produced very good bulbs. The main difference was that the plants raised in the greenhouse matured about three weeks later than those sown in the summer and overwintered.

Optimum Spacing

Growing vegetables at the optimum spacing has an important effect on the yields we can expect from the land available. Like any other plant, vegetables will compete with their neighbours for food, water and light and the availability of these factors will determine the eventual size of the plants. And that generally means the amount of usable produce.

If, for example, you were to grow your onions 1 ft (30 cm.) apart, as many exhibitors do, the chances are that the bulbs would be enormous. But they would not be as big as two onions grown 6 in. (15 cm.) apart. That is perhaps a bit of an over-simplification, but it illustrates the point. You will grow the biggest plants at wide spacings, and the smallest at close spacings, but you will get the biggest yield *per square yard*, at a spacing that just – *only* just – prevents one plant from competing with its neighbour.

For most crops, that theory is fine, and a little experimenting will soon decide which is the optimum spacing.

But sometimes, we may want to use the effects of competition to our advantage. Take pickling onions for example. Here we grow them very close together deliberately, so as to produce bulbs small enough for the purpose. Baby beet are another good example, where the small, tender roots are much to be preferred.

We can also save a considerable amount of waste, by growing vegetables to suit the size and appetites of the family. For a family of two, there is little point in growing massive cabbages, since they would either have to eat cabbage until it was coming out of their ears or throw half of it away. Much better to grow the plants closer together to produce smaller heads that can be eaten all in one meal.

Mini-cauliflowers
The effects of close spacing in producing smaller plants with less waste, was dramatically demonstrated in a trial at Barnsdale using cauliflowers. The method was developed by the NVRS and we found that it worked like a charm.

The idea is to grow summer cauliflowers at such a close spacing, that the curds produced are just the right size to make a meal for one person.

There are several advantages, apart from the sheer convenience of being able to pop the whole head into the pot without preparation. The curds produced are from $1\frac{1}{2}$ to $3\frac{1}{2}$ in. (4–9 cm.) across – just the right size for freezing whole. They look very attractive on the plate with a little sheath of green leaves around the white curd. But above all, the plants produce a much higher proportion of curd compared to leaf, so there is less waste. And, of course, that means more of the usable produce per square yard. In a small garden, that's exactly what we're looking for.

Varieties

It is important to choose the right varieties. The method only works with summer cauliflower, and the varieties musᵗ be ones that give a good uniformity of size and of time to maturity. Since the technique depends upon all the plants developing together, so as to restrict each other's growth, only a few varieties have so far been found suitable. I had the best results from Predominant and Garant, both of which are available through the seed catalogues if you can't find them in the shop.

Both these varieties can be grown in succession to mature from about mid-June to October. Successional sowing is important with this method. Bear in mind that its very essence is to produce all the curds at the same time, so don't get carried away and grow too many at once. Much better grow a small number in each batch, and time the batches to give a succession of harvesting. You may well feel, as I do, that you don't want cauliflower at all in August and September when there is so much more exotic stuff about. But one of the beauties of this method, is that you can almost exactly time your harvesting date from the sowing time.

Sowing

As with all cauliflowers, the preparation of the soil before sowing is of vital importance. The secret of success is to keep the plants growing steadily and uniformly.

Since the plants need to be grown in a block rather than in rows, it is best to prepare a bed. Naturally, this is an ideal subject for deep-bed growing. Fork some organic matter into the soil and before sowing rake in a dressing of Growmore at 4 oz per sq. yd (120 gm per sq. m.).

This will last the plants throughout their lives and there will be no need to apply more. Indeed, too much nitrogen results in excessive leaf growth and poorer quality curds, so too rich a soil is to be avoided.

Make the first sowing towards the end of March or early April. Draw the seed drills in the normal way, about ½ in. (13 mm.) deep and 6 in. (15 cm.) apart. The seeds are sown along the row in 'stations', placing two seeds per station 6 in. (15 cm.) apart (71). Cover the drills and tamp down lightly with the back of a rake.

If the soil is dry, as it may well be with the later sowings during the summer, run a little water in the drill before sowing. This should be the last time the plants need water, since overwatering will also produce an excess of leaves at the expense of curd quality. Naturally though, if the soil

71. *Mini-cauliflowers are sown close together in stations*

becomes very dry to the point where the plants are suffering, water will have to be given.

Cultivation

If two seeds germinate in one station, one of them should be removed as soon as possible. It will be necessary also to remove weeds in the early stages of growth, though later on the plants themselves will swamp them and prevent further growth.

Cauliflowers are very subject to attacks from cabbage root fly so it is essential to take preventative measures. Once the wilting symptoms are seen, it is really too late, so it is better to anticipate an attack. Full details of cabbage root fly control are given on pages 54–55.

It is likely also, that flea beetle will attack the seedlings. These small beetles can do an incredible amount of damage, sometimes completely skeletonising leaves. They are easy to control with an insecticidal dust such as derris or gamma HCH. An alternative method which I have tried with some success, uses no insecticide at all. So, if you are anti-chemical, this one may.be worth giving a go.

The little beetles are called 'flea' beetles because of their habit of jumping high into the air when they are disturbed. This characteristic can be used to catch them. Simply coat a flat board with some old grease, and move it along the row just above the crop. The beetles jump into the air and are caught on the grease. This method does certainly catch a lot of beetles, though I wouldn't like to guarantee 100 per cent success (72).

Aphids and caterpillars must also be controlled. For greenfly it is preferable to use a special greenfly killer – there are several available – and caterpillars can be killed with fenitrothion (Murphy Fentro).

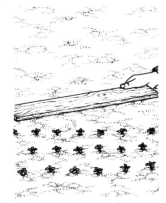

72. *A novel method of controlling flea-beetle*

Harvesting

There is a fairly short period of harvesting with most of the curds maturing at the same time. Keep a close eye on them when they start to show, since they develop quite rapidly. They should not really be allowed to exceed about 3½ in. (9 cm.), or quality will be impaired. Take them off with a knife, cutting below the curd, to leave that attractive sheath of leaves. No further preparation other than washing is needed.

I found in the trials at Barnsdale that the plants in the centre of the block remained small, as they should be, but those on the outside rows with less competition, tended to outgrow them. I still left the outside rows until the remainder had almost matured, to avoid reducing the competition. Otherwise, I felt, those towards the middle of the block might also grow too large. An alternative would have been to sow them only 6 in. (15 cm.) from the neighbouring crop.

I also tried raising the plants in a seed bed, selecting plants of much the same size and transplanting them 6 in. (15 cm.) apart. Even though the plants were carefully graded, they still seemed to develop at different rates, and the method was not really successful. Some curds developed to 5–6 in. (12–15 cm.) across, while others produced hardly any curd at all. There is no doubt that to be really successful, the plants have to be raised from seed sown *in situ*.

Perhaps the only snag with this method is the fact that the curds all mature at once. That's fine if you are growing them specifically for the freezer, but you could otherwise be faced with a glut if you grow too many. The answer is to grow just a few and to sow them at regular intervals to provide a succession of maturity. It must be borne in mind, however, that the plants will take longer to mature when the weather is colder towards the end of the year.

How to make Cheap Cloches

Sensible use of the space available is unquestionably the most effective way to increase the vegetable harvest from a small garden. But there are other factors that will help too. Obviously, we need to choose the heaviest yielding varieties, and we can also try to extend the season, both at the beginning and at the end of the year.

That's easy, of course, if you have a heated greenhouse, (and can afford to run it) but with fuel prices going through the roof we felt that there was a need to investigate alternative methods. The obvious answer is to use cloches to cover early crops and to finish off the ripening of such things as tomatoes, cucumbers and marrows. But even the price of a humble cloche brings me out in a cold sweat, so I've been investigating some alternatives. The aim was to discover the cheapest cloche in the world.

After a year of trials at Barnsdale, I've come up with two interesting answers of which the first is tunnels.

Cheaper tunnels
This, I must admit, is not a new idea. Tunnel cloches, consisting of a series of wire hoops covered with sheet polythene, have been around for years. What we did on *Gardeners' World* was to devise a do-it-yourself model that can be made for a fraction of the cost of a proprietary brand.

To start with, it is best to make what engineers call, I believe, a 'jig'. This is simply a piece of equipment that is easy to make yourself and produces frame after frame, all exactly the same. It is certainly possible to bend the wires individually but it's a time-consuming process, and they never come out looking the same. This means that your tunnel will vary in height and possibly width, right the way down the line. The plants underneath it won't mind but it looks untidy and will grate on your eye every time you take a walk round the garden.

Making the jig is simplicity itself. Get yourself a piece of wood 1½ in. × 1 in. (4 cm. × 2.5 cm.) thick and cut it to 4 ft 6 in (1.3 m.) long. You'll also need a couple of stout bolts.

Drill the wood and put in the first bolt, 6 in. (15 cm.) from one end. The second bolt goes 3 ft (91 cm.) from that or 1 ft (30 cm.) from the other end. Now mark a clear line 6 in. (15 cm.) from that bolt, and you have your jig. Simple really.

To make the wire frames you'll need some 12 gauge galvanised wire and this is the most expensive part of the operation. Still, a small roll of wire will make a lot of cloches.

Use the jig first of all to measure and cut off a 4 ft 6 in. (1.3 m.) length of wire. Now you need to clamp the jig onto a firm base. I used one of those portable benches which was ideal but you could clamp it to the kitchen table, or even nail it to the fence.

Put one end of the wire level with the line you marked on the wood and twist it round the first bolt. This will leave 6 in. (15 cm.) before the twist, to make one leg of the cloche. Now twist round the other bolt, which will automatically leave 6 in. (15 cm.) for the other leg. Remove the wire from the jig and you have your cloche frame.

Mark out the position of the tunnel on the ground with two tight garden lines 18 in. (45 cm.) apart, and then simply push the legs in on the lines and about 3 ft (90 cm.) apart. The wires will all assume the same curve automatically, to look neat and tidy. The loop in the wires should be just above soil level.

The best thing to use for the cover is a sheet of polythene sold as a replacement cover for the proprietary tunnel cloches. They are not expensive, and can be found at most good gardening shops.

Bang in a stout stake at the end of the row of cloches and fix one end of the polythene to it, simply by wrapping it round and tying off. The cover can now be stretched over the row of wire hoops and tied in the same fashion at the other end.

To make the polythene really tight and windproof tie a piece of strong string to one of the loops in the wire supports, run it over the top of the tunnel and fix it to the other side, stretching it as tightly as you can. This will hold the polythene tight, while still enabling you to lift the side for watering or weeding.

The resulting tunnel is very effective in raising early crops and a fraction of the shop price.

Slitted polythene for increased yields

Even cheaper than my home-made tunnel cloches, is a new material that is simply sheet polythene perforated by thousands of small slits. I tested it at Barnsdale with some startling results and I have also made use of the results of similar trials carried out by Fisons at their Levington research station. With some exceptions it increased final yields and brought most crops on quite a bit earlier.

The principle is so simple that, like all good ideas, it makes you wonder why no one thought of it before. By some ingenious manufacturing method the polythene is slitted at regular intervals, so that when the material is stretched, the slits open. Unstretched, they close back again.

To use it, the crops are covered immediately after sowing or planting. As the plants grow they push up the polythene and open the slits, thus gradually hardening themselves off and allowing rain water to get to the soil beneath.

73. *Before sowing or planting apply the necessary amount of fertiliser*

65

74. *Rake the fertiliser in a fortnight before planting*

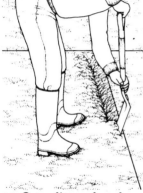

75. *Cut a slit trench at the edge of the bed*

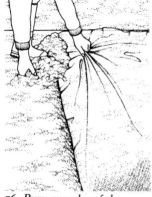

76. *Bury one edge of the polythene in the trench*

Once the slits are fully open the sheet can be removed and re-used on another crop.

Inevitably there were disadvantages, but on the whole the system worked well. The two biggest problems were slugs, and weeds. Both do extremely well under the polythene sheeting, and they must be diligently controlled. After sowing or planting I used methiocarb slug pellets which gave complete control.

Weeds were not so easy. The first experiment at Barnsdale failed miserably, because we did not allow for a dramatic increase in weed growth. The sheeting was used to cover broad beans – which I now think is not the ideal subject. When it was removed, the crop was completely hidden by a verdant jungle of weed-growth and was suffering. A couple of rows of beans alongside, that were not covered, produced a better crop.

The reason for my failure to keep the crop weed-free lay in the method of anchoring the sheeting. I had buried it in a 3 in. (7.5 cm.) slit in the soil, on all four sides. A better method is to bury one side only and to hold the other three sides by weighting them down with bricks, or with special pegs made for the job (79).

The crop can then be inspected from time to time and weeded if necessary. I also noticed some damage to vegetables with pointed heads. Pointed varieties of cabbage and lettuce were most affected. However, there was no such damage to round-headed varieties. I also found the material to be unsuitable for onions. They tended to grow through the slits, and were badly damaged when the sheeting was removed. However, the trial at Levington produced quite different results. There the final yield of onions was increased by as much as 30 per cent.

Though it is claimed that the material will last for several seasons, my own feeling was that it was too flimsy to be used over and over again. I therefore decided to make the maximum use of it in the first year.

By careful planning, it is possible to cover an early crop and, when it is time to remove it, simply to turn it over without removing the side that is buried in the soil, to cover an adjacent crop. This worked well with such things as lettuce, beetroot or carrots, followed by marrows, courgettes, cucumbers or bush tomatoes. The permutations are endless.

It is quite important to uncover the crops at the right time, and in the following details of the vegetables tried, I have indicated the length of time they were covered. Often the sheeting is there just to reduce the danger of frost damage to early crops, and there seems to be little advantage in continuing the protection once the danger has passed. Certainly, when the polythene will stretch no more it must be removed.

Beetroot
A crop of Avonearly beetroot was sown in early March and covered with the sheeting for 12 weeks – the time it took for the beet to mature. They were harvested as baby-beet quite a bit earlier than a crop sown outside at the same time, and the total yield was about 4 per cent heavier. This was one of the more notable successes.

Cabbage
Cabbage Derby Day, a round-headed variety, was covered for 6 weeks and the yield was increased by about 20 per cent, as well as being earlier. This was the only variety of cabbage I tried, but at Levington the pointed variety Hispi was damaged by contact with the polythene. They also suffered slug damage which did not occur at Barnsdale, no doubt because of our use of methiocarb.

77. *Plant or sow in the bed*

Carrots
Early carrots, variety Amsterdam Forcing, were sown in early March and covered for 6 weeks. The crop was considerably increased and was earlier too. Just at a time when the last of the maincrop carrots from store were finishing, I was able to pull the first of the new crop.

At Levington, maincrop carrots were also tried and these too produced an earlier, heavier crop. They also noted a definite reduction in carrot fly damage, so it would seem that pests find it difficult to penetrate the material.

Lettuce
The variety Tom Thumb was sown in early March and covered for 6 weeks. As expected, there was no increase in yield, because a lettuce will grow to maximum size and then stop anyway. But the fact that I was cutting good heads a couple of weeks before the outside crop made it very worthwhile. Later in the season, there was little advantage in covering lettuce, since it does not increase the yield.

Pointed-headed varieties like Lobjoits Green were quite badly damaged by the film and should be avoided.

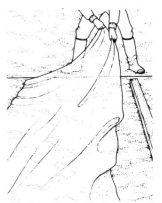

78. *Carefully pull the polythene over the sown soil*

Onion
I tried growing onion Hygro under slitted polythene at Barnsdale but with little success. The thin shoots pushed their way through the slits, and when the sheet was removed, the plants were virtually destroyed. However, at Levington, they recorded an increase of 10 per cent and 30 per cent on two different varieties.

Potato
It is always difficult to judge the right time to plant potato seed for the earliest crop. The aim is to judge it so that the first shoots do not emerge until after the danger of frost. Obviously this varies from year to year, so the process can be

79. *Anchor the edges with wood or brick*

nothing but hit-or-miss. Under slitted polythene, the tubers can be set much earlier, because the young shoots will be protected from light frosts.

I planted Maris Bard under the sheeting in early March, and dug my first potatoes a couple of weeks earlier than those planted at the same time uncovered. The shoots of these had in fact been damaged by frost, which sets them back considerably.

The same varieties planted in late March were also a couple of weeks later, so this is certainly a useful application.

The crop was uncovered when the danger of hard frost was past in late May and the sheeting was then turned over to protect courgettes, enabling me to plant a fortnight earlier, and get a first picking also two weeks before those planted at the normal time.

Sweet Corn

For the gardener without a greenhouse, sweet corn sown outside is always a risky business. If the weather is not conducive to early ripening it is quite possible that, despite all efforts, the cobs simply do not ripen. The plants need a full season in which to do this, so early sowing under glass, and planting out in early June, is the only sure way. Direct sowing and then covering with slitted polythene, however, solved the problem. The seed was sown in mid-May and covered for just 4 weeks, after coming off a crop of early lettuce. The plants flowered earlier than those sown outside without covering, and produced a higher yield of ripe cobs.

Polythene mulches – how to avoid weeds

Slitted polythene is also available in black for use as a mulch, so I tried this as well in two ways.

First of all, it can be laid down between rows of plants right up to the stems. Here it will reduce weeding to a minimum and will also serve to prevent evaporation of water from the surface of the soil. One of the best applications for this was between rows of runner beans. It is always quite a problem to clean in between the canes, especially when the crop grows up. In the middle of the season it is impossible to wield a hoe in the confined space without causing damage to the crop. If the polythene is laid down between the two rows of canes before planting and weighted with stones, there should be no need to weed the area at all for the rest of the season.

I did find, in fact, that a few weeds managed to push their way through the slits but this was on such a limited scale that it was never a problem.

The second way the material was used, was to plant through it. This time it was laid out first on a prepared strip of ground and all four edges were buried about 3 in.

(7.5 cm.) in the soil. A cross was cut in the sheeting at the appropriate spacings to make a hole big enough to plant through.

The cross must be cut so that the lines of the two cuts run at an angle to the slits. Otherwise the material is liable to tear, and once it does, it can 'run' just like a laddered stocking.

This method was most effective in keeping down weeds, though some did manage to struggle through immediately round the plants. They were no trouble to pull out by hand.

This method can also be used in conjunction with the clear cover, so that it should not have to be raised at all until it is time to uncover. However, there is one big danger. Our old friend the slug is at his happiest in the moist, dark conditions created by the polythene mulch. It is *essential* to use a slug killer under the sheet whether you normally have a slug problem or not. If slugs already cause headaches, it may be better not to use the mulch.

There could be one other disadvantage with black polythene mulches, though I must say that this is a factor I haven't tested. It is possible that the sheeting could have the effect of lowering soil temperatures just a little. On most crops this would have little effect in late spring and summer, but on such subjects as sweet corn, it could delay germination.

Some crops – sweet corn, marrows, courgettes, cucumbers, melons etc. – are very sensitive to soil temperatures, particularly during germination, so it is perhaps best to avoid the use of black sheeting for these vegetables if they are direct sown.

Index